Listening Well

Bringing Stories of Hope to Life

HEATHER
MORRIS

ST. MARTIN'S PRESS
NEW YORK

First published in the United States by St. Martin's Press,
an imprint of St. Martin's Publishing Group

www.stmartins.com

Library of Congress Cataloging-in-Publication Data

Names: Morris, Heather (Screenwriter), author.
Title: Listening well : bringing stories of hope to life / Heather
    Morris.
Description: First U.S. edition. | New York : St. Martin's Press,
    2022.
Identifiers: LCCN 2022005282 | ISBN 9781250276919
    (hardcover) | ISBN 9781250276926 (ebook)
Subjects: LCSH: Morris, Heather (Screenwriter) | Authors,
    New Zealand—21st century—Biography. | Listening
    (Philosophy) | LCGFT: Autobiographies.
Classification: LCC PR9639.4.M668 Z46 2022 | DDC
    823/.92 [B]—dc23/eng/20220203
LC record available at https://lccn.loc.gov/2022005282

Our books may be purchased in bulk for promotional,
educational, or business use. Please contact your local bookseller or
the Macmillan Corporate and Premium Sales Department at
1-800-221-7945, extension 5442, or by email at
MacmillanSpecialMarkets@macmillan.com.

Originally published in the United Kingdom by Manilla Press,
an imprint of Bonnier Books UK

First U.S. Edition: 2022

10 9 8 7 6 5 4 3 2 1

To Christopher Charles Berry, my great-grandfather, the person who first showed me how to listen.

To the first responders around the world who are bravely fighting to keep us safe, giving us the hope we need during this pandemic for a brighter, better future.

To the staff, patients, and their families I was honored to work with and engage with during my time at Monash Medical Centre in Melbourne. You showed me how to care.

Contents

Contents

Introduction

January 1, 2020. A new day dawns, a new year, a new decade. A sense of hope for us, individually and collectively as a global community, that it will be a "good year." In the words of Lale Sokolov, my dear friend and the man whose extraordinary story I told in *The Tattooist of Auschwitz*: "If you wake up in the morning, it is a good day." Resolutions, both new and repeated from previous years, are made, perhaps whispered to our nearest and dearest. If we share our hopes and dreams for the year, they stand a better chance of happening, we are told.

The fireworks from the previous night, whether watched live or on a television set, have burned out, the parties have packed up, hangovers are being nursed in a variety of ways. I live in Melbourne, on the east coast of Australia. This year, our celebrations were tempered, our fireworks did not go off in many places. We still made our wishes, hopes, and dreams known, but these too were tempered. All of us were concerned about the bushfires that had started a week or so earlier and which were still far from being under control. In fact, they got worse. Much worse.

Over the next week towns were razed, people lost their lives, their homes, their communities. The impact on flora and fauna was devastating. Images went around the world of Australia's two most iconic symbols—kangaroos and koalas—becoming the symbols of destruction and despair. New Zealand, Canada, and the United States sent firefighters to help in what was fast becoming a national disaster. Three did not return home to their families—they were killed when their plane went down during a water-bombing mission.

Celebrities around the world made considerable donations to help those affected. Small children gave up their summer holidays to sell cookies in the street, anything to help raise funds. The Royal Family sent their thoughts and prayers. Artists from around the world came to Australia, putting on the biggest live entertainment concert ever seen here. Millions and millions of dollars were handed over to the firefighters and to the charities set up to help those impacted.

For several weeks it seemed nothing could stop this monstrous blaze as smaller ones joined, charging from the mountains to the sea. Prepare for the worst, hope for the best. In this case, the best was rainfall of biblical proportions. We all prayed for rain. And eventually, that is what happened. The heavens opened and for days it rained, helping to extinguish many of the fires. The deluge on parched soil also wrought havoc, causing mudslides in areas weakened by the loss of ground-stabilizing trees. Floods now ravaged small towns, killing the domestic livestock, destroying more homes.

The events in Australia in January 2020 resonated around the world, not because they don't happen anywhere else, but because Australia's southern hemisphere summer made it the only country burning as the new decade began. The northern hemisphere was still recovering from its own summer of hell. But worse was to come. It was during this strange and unsettling time that we first heard the word coronavirus, or COVID-19.

Since then, the world has changed beyond measure, beyond belief, beyond comprehension. We have all faced a pandemic of unknown proportions; the worst experienced by anyone alive today. It has brought stress levels to us individually and collectively like never before. Loss of jobs. Divorce. Illness that many may take a long time, if ever, to recover from. Death. With modern media, both conventional and social, few stories of tragedy go unreported. They are there, 24/7, for us to turn away from, then find ourselves turning back, such is our need to watch disasters unfold. We have pulled together, but sadly, we have also pulled apart. Curling up in the fetal position may be the only way some of us can blot out the pain of suffering emotionally, in our health, economically.

We have tried to take care of each other. After all, we are pack animals in a sense, drawn to human connection and contact. We have looked for joy in our changed living conditions. The smile of a young child oblivious to the pain of survival can be a huge tonic during an emotional low. The need to get out of bed and feed a pet has been for many of us what gets us through the day. Isolation can and has had a devastating effect on many of us. Where is my pack? Where is my tribe? Remember this: they are there, like you, waiting for the day when we can say, "We got through this together. We are stronger." The wave of memes reminding us that our grandfathers fought a war for us while all we are being asked to do is sit on the sofa and watch Netflix makes a mockery of the real trauma of being forced to isolate for so many people. As Lale always said to me, "All you have to do is wake up in the morning." Maybe we are now being asked to wake up in more ways than one.

Could this be our planet telling us to slow down? Has she not been screaming out to us for decades to take better care of her? How many warnings must she give us before we start listening to her? Many already have. In nearly every country there has been an ongoing battle, gathering force in the past couple of years, between governments and scientists over the impact of climate change. Amazing and inspiring activists, both young and old, are rallying the cause, telling those in power, telling all of us, that it's time to shut up and listen to our planet.

COVID-19 is a common enemy that does not discriminate over religion, politics, gender orientation, race, or age and its effects are being felt across the world. And yet in the face of this unknown, new enemy, the changes we are making are having unexpected and positive benefits. Within only a few weeks of this crisis, we received reports of cleaner air and a reduction in pollution levels across China and many European cities. As we were forced inside, the skies became clearer, the rivers ran cleaner. We could look outside at what awaited us.

As I write this, I look out my window onto my street. Today, I see not cars and vans but people. Men and women, all ages, alone, together, many with young children, even more accompanied by dogs. They walk the street, they talk; I can tell. They listen. Their dogs bark at other dogs hidden from view by fences, their presence still being made known. Keeping their social distance, they acknowledge each other. Many stop and chat briefly. What do these interactions tell me? For the first time in living memory, we have a common purpose. A common enemy which will be defeated by us all doing our bit.

At the height of the lockdown, I watched as a van pulled up outside a nearby house and a young girl took from the back a box, filled with groceries. I smiled at the Hollywood scene of a French stick of bread poking out the top. I watched as she knocked on the door, placed the box on the porch, and stepped back. The elderly woman living in the house must have seen her coming, as the door opened immediately. I heard her saying, "Thank you, thank you," over and over. I heard the emotion in her voice. If I had needed to speak at that moment, I would have struggled. With a big smile and a "You are very welcome, I'll see you in two days' time," the girl danced back to the van.

Reflecting on this scene, I found myself thinking not about the elderly woman, but the young girl. Was she volunteering because she had lost her job? Was she a university student now denied her studies? Where had the groceries come from that she was handing out? Donated, or had she paid for them herself?

We can never know what is going on in other people's—other than our families' and friends'—lives. What makes someone carry out acts of compassion and generosity? What makes them act out, lash out, even abuse people trying to help them? I have seen this reaction many times, working in a hospital. My daughter and son-in-law, both police officers, see it too many times. Once again, I am reminded never to judge until you have walked a mile in someone's shoes. Midway through the year, the brutal murder of George Floyd by a police officer in the United

States ignited a wave of anger and the demand for recognition that black lives matter across the world. I am reminded of Lale's words to me: "It does not matter what color your skin, your religion, your ethnicity, your sexual orientation. We all bleed the same color." He got it. We are, all of us, human beings.

Right now, it is even difficult to offer our services as volunteers due to the need to keep our distance. Many want to, need to, reach out and help where they can. Isolation for people living alone is particularly hard until such time as that young girl I saw can enter the home of the elderly woman, help her unpack her groceries and put them away, maybe have a cup of tea and a chat with her. To be denied intimate contact is particularly hard—people need physical contact, a hug or a kiss from a beloved friend, family member, grandchild.

We are all going to have to take a step back, to hold our tongues in the coming months, maybe years, as we adjust to the impact of COVID-19. Unemployment and the associated issues it brings are already a major problem in all countries. Some career paths may not return, new forms of study and work will need to be sought. The impact on families will be immense, as we know from the Great Depression. However, we also know we can adjust, that we can seek out a different way of life. It may not be the same as it was, it may be better. Our global outlook will probably shrink for a while into the community and neighborhood we live in. That need not be a bad thing. As we reconnect and share our individual stories of how we coped during the pandemic of 2020, we will listen and learn, we will laugh and cry. It will be a new world and in many ways it will be a darker world, but it may also be a better one. This is a time to accept whatever lies ahead, to avoid nostalgia for the past and be open to the inevitable change that lies ahead for all of us.

However, can we not breathe in the fresh air and ask whether our industries do better when coming back online, to slow down their emissions with the aim of eliminating them altogether? If we can be smart enough to fight COVID-19, we can be smart enough to take this opportunity to strive for a cleaner planet. The extent to which COVID-19 is directly connected to climate change is gradually becoming clearer, and in a very short space of time we have opened our eyes to how quickly we can create a cleaner, safer environment. Perhaps it's time for us all to stop and listen to what our planet is showing us. It can be repaired, but it can't do it alone: we who inhabit it must work with it. We must listen to our planet.

Listening Well explores listening; how through listening to others we will find inspiration in the everyday lives of those around us.

The day I met Lale Sokolov, a few weeks after the death of his wife, he told me he hoped he could stay alive long enough to tell me his story. He didn't want to be with me, he said every time I knocked on his door, he wanted to be with Gita. Those were the words he said to me each day, until the day he said he now hoped he could live for as long as it took for him to talk, for me to listen, so I could write his story.

I had no qualifications for this. What I did possess, though I didn't think about it at the time, was my ability to listen. Truly, actively listen. Daily, I went to work in the social work department of a large Melbourne hospital. There, I engaged with patients, family members, carers, other hospital professionals: they spoke, I listened. Often, they didn't know what to say, or *how* to say what they were thinking, feeling—yes, feeling more than thinking. It didn't matter. By staying quiet, letting them know I wasn't going anywhere, that I was there to listen, help if I could, often they found enough words. It was a privilege to be the person a stranger found themselves talking to and occasionally being able to make a small difference to their lives at a time of tragedy or trauma.

Now that privilege of hearing stories is sent to me by readers of *The Tattooist of Auschwitz, Cilka's Journey*, and *Three Sisters*. I am in awe of the outpouring of emotion shared with me, touched by the knowledge that telling Lale and Cecilia "Cilka" Klein's stories has connected with so many, that reading their stories has had a profound impact on men and women, old and young, across the world and helped them in a dark moment of their lives. I sincerely hope that in writing to me and sharing the hope they have of waking up the next day, and the next, I continue to make a small difference. I don't get to see or touch my readers, but I often put faces to them, picture them and the surroundings they describe. While reading people's letters, I am listening to them too.

I have come to realize that listening is an art and my hope is that through reading this book, you may also decide to practice it more actively. I can promise if you do, you will be changed by the stories you hear—and changed for the better. Only by hearing their stories can we empathize with others, give them a voice, give them hope that someone else cares. We need to meet their courage in opening up and sharing their vulnerability with compassion and we must encourage them to do so again.

As you read on, I will share with you what it was like for me to listen to my beloved great-grandfather and the wisdom and fun that can come from listening to our elders. I will also talk about the importance of listening to children. I am a mother and a grandmother, and while I do not claim to have been the perfect parent (my children would agree!), I do think that I learned a thing or two from listening to my children and recognizing the validity of their thoughts and feelings, no matter how small or trivial they may have seemed at the time. I will share with you more stories of my time with Lale and what listening to this rare soul has taught me, as well as what I have learned from the many others who have found the courage to tell me stories of deeply personal and emotional periods in their lives. And I will also share with you the hardest lesson of all that I have learned: that above all, you need to listen to *yourself*.

In this book, I want to offer you some thoughts on how to listen actively. If you listen and learn, you just might find yourself in the position of offering hope to others. There is no beginning and there is no end in the circle of accepting and sharing these stories. No one has ownership of them, and no one's experiences in life are more valid than another's. They are unique to the individual, but by listening to them we can *all* become a little wiser, a little bit more compassionate and understanding, and we can enrich our own lives through what others have to tell us about theirs.

Other than a lifetime's experience, I have no credentials for advising anyone on how to live their life or what paths to follow when confronted with more than one, nor do I subscribe to any faith or religion. All I can offer are lessons learned from my own personal good fortune in finding others prepared to tell me their stories—and my willingness to listen to them. Simple? Yes, it is. Try it.

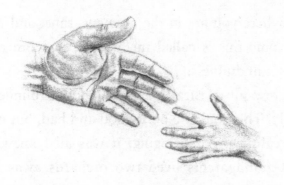

1

Listening to the Wisdom
of Our Elders

*Listen to your elders' advice not because they
are always right, but because they have more
experiences of being wrong.*

Girly. He called me "Girly." He was my great-grandfather and he taught me how to listen. Not just
to him or other humans, but to the sounds around
us: animals, birds, machines—or just nothing. Some-times in life there can be nothing sweeter than the
sound of silence. If you let it in, you might just find
yourself centered, rested, comfortable in who you are

and where you are in the moment, time, and place. For some this is called meditation; in more recent times, mindfulness.

I grew up in rural New Zealand surrounded by family. This could be both good and bad, but it was my reality, my upbringing, it was all I knew. My great-grandparents lived two orchards away from the home I shared with my parents and four brothers. I was the second-born, two years and two days after my oldest brother. The three boys that followed I considered an annoyance to be ignored. Pirongia, the place where I lived, cannot be called a town, not even a village. The mountain the area was named after ruled over us, its slopes, forest, rivers, and streams my backyard. It is where I would escape to, often with my oldest brother. The area was dairy country, cows ruled our lives. The twice-daily milking, calving, everything bovine, was part of our DNA. They remain my favorite animal. Self-sufficient in all food groups, what we didn't grow, a neighbor did, and we exchanged produce. We also exchanged labor with our neighbors. Some of my fondest memories are being at a neighbor's house as my father, along with the other local men, got together to bale hay, plant—in general, help out where needed.

Years later, when I watched the movie *Witness*, a story set among the Amish people in the US, I flashed back to my childhood. It was the same. Neighbor helping neighbor, minus any religious affiliations. I never minded every school holiday being packed off to a relative to help work their farm. I had an uncle and aunt who lived about two hours away, ran a sheep station and had five daughters. Here, gender meant nothing, as we girls pulled our weight with the men. Riding horses, we rounded up sheep spread over thousands of acres, ushered them into the race to be "dipped" in (dunking them in insecticides), then into the pens to be shorn.

My other escape was school. With only four classrooms and fewer than fifty students covering Years 1–6, my friends were limited, gender played no part in who you befriended. With the majority of children coming and going from school by bus, playing with friends after school was not an option. My brothers and I walked to school; no bus came our way. The joy of walking in winter, when the puddles alongside the poorly made road were covered in ice, gave me immense pleasure. I'd use the heel of my shoe to shatter the ice, often meaning I'd then spend the rest of the day in wet shoes and socks.

Men were men. Women were, well, women, but not

the kind of woman I intended to be. There is nothing wrong with being a stay-at-home mother and home-maker if that's what you want to do. However, in the 1950s and '60s, women like my mother, my aunties, and other local women I knew only ever complained about their lot in life. They envied their men, though I don't know why—they worked all hours of the day and night and seemed as sad and unfulfilled as the women. The only difference I recall was that the men didn't bother complaining. I need to repeat: I was living in rural New Zealand—I cannot say how it was for the Kiwi women in large towns and cities.

I am so proud of New Zealand. From being the first country in the world to give women the vote, it has had three female prime ministers since 1997, which is a superb achievement. Dame Jenny Shipley and Helen Clark led the way to the current incumbent, Jacinda Ardern. Jacinda embodies everything needed in a leader, particularly at this point in time when we are all living under the pandemic, COVID-19. Her compassion, her empathy, and the way she listens to the people of her country makes her the envy of many other nations: she is seen, she is heard, she listens.

Children should be seen and not heard. This was

the backstory to my childhood. Except for one person, my great-grandfather. Sadly, on reflection, no other family member wanted to hear from us children and certainly didn't want to listen to anything we might have to say; they never took much time to speak to us, certainly not at the level of imparting advice or wisdom. Except for my great-grandfather—and if you could get him on his own and he was in the mood, occasionally my quiet, thoughtful father as well.

Then there was my mother. I am told all mother/daughter relationships are complicated. Mine, I would describe as practically nonexistent. Other than to tell me to do something, she seldom spoke to me. Affection was absent, and I balked at being told to clean up after my brothers, make their school lunches. Do the domestic chores and do them without complaining. She followed in the footsteps of her mother and my widowed grandmother, who lived directly across a small road from us. Cousins, uncles, and aunties also lived not too far away. Extended family scattered in the small village.

From the age of about ten, I was instructed to stop off at my great-grandparents' house on my way home from school to see if there was anything they needed.

My mother would have already been over and left them their evening meal to be heated up. I always found my great-grandmother inside, either pottering in the kitchen, or later, as her health deteriorated, in bed. She never had much to say to me. She looked at me with an expression of pity, a look I also received from my grandmother and mother. I was a girl. My mother had told me many times she was sorry she had me, that being a girl I was doomed to a life of hard work, limited freedom. My brothers were the lucky ones and would have the world to explore, choices where I had none.

As a teenager, I recall my mother making comments about one or two local boys she thought I should spend more time with. I didn't understand what she meant—I saw them as much as I wanted to. They were OK to spend time with one day, but I wanted nothing to do with them the next. On one occasion, she told me I was having dinner at a neighbor's place. We never went out to dinner. Occasionally, when the men were working on a neighbor's farm, as families we would gather there and share a meal, but to be told I was going to dinner, alone, was unheard of. When I asked her why, I was told it was so I could spend some time with one of their sons and get to know the family better. I had known them all my life, what more was there to know? But I was told I was going and that was that. I confided in my older brother, who was a close friend of the boy, asking him what he knew. Never one to hold back, he told me our mothers had considered we should get together; it would be a good fit for our families if we married. So I did as I was told, and went to dinner with the boy's family. His mother was a better cook than mine.

But within a year, as soon as I had saved enough money, I fled to Australia. I was not quite eighteen. Until I subsequently married and produced a grandchild, my mother did not feature in my life. It helped that I was in another country. Even after I produced two more grandchildren, gained a university degree as a mature student, and got a good job, she still wrote to me as Mrs. (my husband's first name) Morris. No emotional or personal conversations ever took place. In retrospect, I know how lucky I was to have one person in my life as a young girl who talked to me: Gramps, my great-grandfather.

Regardless of the weather, I would find Gramps sitting on the back veranda in a big comfy armchair put there just for him, a small stool for his feet to rest on in front of him. Next to him was Grandma's chair, though I rarely saw her sitting in it—perhaps she did during the day when I was at school.

As I came out of the kitchen door onto the veranda, the slamming of the screen door would make him turn his head. You know, his face always lit up when he saw me and he would pat Grandma's chair, which was my indication to sit. Minutes would pass before he spoke. We both looked down the backyard with its giant chestnut tree to the right, the vegetable garden to the left, the paddock with the "house cow" grazing next to it, the outbuildings, sheds, garage to the rear and the gate and path that I would take through two orchards to my home. Next to the chestnut tree, a prized persimmon tree threatened its neighbor for dominance. As the leaves changed color, heralding the end of summer, the fruit on the persimmon tree would reach its peak. A persimmon is only edible if picked to eat when it is so ripe, it is nearly rotten—otherwise it immediately removes all moisture from the mouth.

Now, persimmon was my great-grandmother's favorite fruit and it was up to Gramps to ensure she got the lot. However, the local birdlife also rated the persimmons highly. At the appointed hour in the ripening of the fruit, Gramps would tie several pieces of rope to strategic branches, attaching a cowbell to each one. The other ends of the rope, running the length of the backyard some one hundred meters, were tied to the arm of his veranda chair. I can only presume he was required to sit there all day for several weeks as the battle for the persimmons was played out between him and the birds. As I sat with him after school, our conversation was peppered with the jangling of cowbells as he yanked on his end of the rope anytime a passing bird so much as slowed down. Often, he would ask me to pull on a particular rope and we would dissolve into giggles as I delayed the tug, letting the birds get close so they would scatter, having passed an unseen line in the sky. This was precision timing at its best. Can I add, no birds were harmed in our protection of the persimmons and I was in my happy place sitting with Gramps.

He was the only person who asked me, "How was school, was it worth going?" Often, I would reply, "No, learned nothing new today," whether I had or not. I didn't want to talk about my day, I was waiting to listen to whatever story he was going to tell me. But at the same time, I was always grateful that he asked, because it told me that he cared. I would sit still, hold my breath, and wait for him to start talking, for the magic to begin.

Often my afternoon time with Gramps would be a

show-and-tell. He would have at the ready an artifact, something he was going to tell me about. Sometimes it was a precious postcard with gold leaves on it, faded writing, that he had brought back from the Boer War in South Africa. He had a spear he told me was a Zulu weapon; he would guide me in handling it, the tip still sharp and threatening. As I did so, in awe of holding something connected to history, to a place so far from where I was sitting, Gramps would go quiet and stare off into the nearby paddock. I would hold it until he came back to me, smiled, and took it from me. When it came to answering my questions of how and where he got it, he would shut down with the words, "It was a terrible time. War is a terrible thing."

When it came to other objects relating to our history, our past with the Maori, he was more talkative. These had been given to him as gifts. As such, he was very happy to share where, when, and from whom he had been given them. I knew what an honor it was to be entrusted with whatever precious object he was speaking about and I'd hold it carefully, turning it this way and that as he spoke. It was spellbinding. Many of these objects were donated to the local museum and I recall seeing them there as a young adult with the small piece of cardboard attached, noting the objects were on loan from his family—that was me, *I* was his family.

No one else in our family trusted me with anything precious. When my great-grandmother grew frail and became bedridden, as the good girl I was I would stop by and see her on my way to school and read her the headlines in the local paper, which would have been delivered the previous day. On her dressing table she had several pieces of jewelry, a brooch or two, some beads, and in a small box a set of double-strung pearls. Standing from sitting on the edge of her bed, I would run the pearls through my fingers before I slowly left the room. She watched me like a hawk, every day saying the same thing: "Don't touch my pearls." But every day, I did. It was like a game between us. When she died a few years later, my grandmother gave me a box one day, saying, "Here, she wanted you to have these." It was the box with the pearls in it. I still have it. Restrung, they are still worn.

Now I know that giving physical objects meaning and importance is interwoven into our culture. When we are small, a teddy bear or a soft blanket becomes what therapists call a transitional object—a physical representation of a caregiver, which becomes imbued with a sense of safety and represents that person when they are not there, enabling the child to sleep alone or be away from home. Later, for all of us, objects will remind us powerfully of a place or time. They can become incredibly comforting reminders of positive experiences—of people, places, memories. I have my great-grandmother's pearls. It is not her they remind me of, but my great-grandfather. In the elderly, they become a bridge back to the past. With Gramps, it was a form of shorthand—he'd pass over the object silently and I'd know that he was going to speak about it; there was no need for him to say, "Shall I tell you about the time . . . ?" And because of who he was, his shyness and diffidence, I knew not to badger or ask for a particular thing, that I had to follow where he wanted to go. These objects were precious, sacrosanct, and there was trauma there too—so somehow I knew that he had to be ready to speak about a particular object and I could only hope I'd get to see those things that interested me. I knew instinctively to wait in the moment, for him to find his way.

I remember the objects so clearly, even now. There was a large greenstone Maori adze (axe), a *toki* in their language, and a Maori feathered cloak. These had been given to him by the local Kākahu Chief. Pirongia, where we lived, was previously called Alexandra.

The New Zealand Wars (the conflict between the Crown and the Maori people over land ownership) had been fought nearby. The relationship between Pakeha (white person) and Maori remained complex for decades. It was not complicated for Gramps—he befriended, worked with, and lived within Maori communities. The respect was mutual and was instrumental in his understanding of and connection to Maori culture, which he shared with me. I was a frequent and welcome visitor to the local Marae, Mātakitaki Pā.

There were also two letters written by Lord Kitchener to Gramps's parents from South Africa, explaining how he was looking after their under-age son who had found himself in a war that he should never have been in. Gramps's parents, my great-grandparents, must have been so proud to receive those letters and so terrified for their son, on another continent—a place they would have known little about.

I sat and held these precious objects and I listened. Never interrupted unless he asked me a question. I never felt he was trying to trick me when he asked questions, a feeling I often had with teachers and my parents—*prove to me you have been listening*. When Gramps asked me why I thought the British were fighting in South Africa and I responded, "I don't know, nothing you have told me explains it," he would smile, nod, and say, "That's because I don't know either and I was there." He once said he hoped I would be able to figure it out and tell him. It was also extremely important to him that I understood the battles fought in the very district we lived in between the Maori and the British. That the British had no right to come to this beautiful country and think they could take it over. He was proud of the Maori for fighting back, as he put it, and chasing the buggers back to England. I always felt my answers were respected, never, ever criticized, just a simple nod of the head that he'd heard me. Why wouldn't I want to listen to him?

Many times, after he'd told me a story, he would stop and say, "Just sit with me and listen." We'd sit there and at first, I'd think we were listening to silence. But then I'd start to tune in to the sounds around me, sounds so familiar I almost didn't hear them: birds, the farm dogs barking in the distance, Grandma clanging dishes and pots, sometimes cussing; Daisy the house cow, waiting for my mother to come and milk her, bellowing in her paddock. And then there were those wonderful moments when there really was silence, just the sound of my own beating heart and his heavy breathing.

Those were the times when I would look up at this big, beautiful old man and see his eyes shut, a smile on his face, and his breathing would be quiet and steady. I would close my eyes and listen to the nothing and feel that he and I were saying something very profound to each other. On rare, even more special occasions, I would feel his hand being placed on mine and I'd be filled with pleasure as we sat as one until something intruded, some sound that would bring us both back from wherever we had been, or Grandma would appear on the back porch and the spell would be broken. She inevitably told me to hurry on home. I would look to Gramps for his reaction. It would vary from "Off you go, Girly" to telling his wife to go back inside as we hadn't finished our time together. The times he made this statement made me feel like the most important person in the world. This revered, respected elder—not only in my family but in our community (he had several stints as Mayor of Pirongia)—wanted to be with me.

He ended our time together each day in the same way, by telling me that if people just stop talking and listen, they will learn more: "Now run along, Girly, I'll see you tomorrow." He knew I would be back. Not because of any sense of family duty but because I wanted to spend time with him. He dwarfed me when we stood together. My younger brothers were afraid of him because of his size. To me it made him all the more my protector—he was a true gentle giant.

We weren't an affectionate family, so I never kissed him or reached out to him. He alone initiated the moments we would touch, by placing his hand over mine.

I used to run everywhere as a child, but leaving Gramps, I would walk as slowly as I could down his garden, through the gate, and along the path through the orchards, reluctant to acknowledge that our time was at an end, dawdling, knowing what awaited me. As I got closer to our house, the sound of my brothers fighting—as boys do—and my mother yelling at them futilely as they became rougher and rougher, would envelop me. No one was listening here, not to each other, and certainly not to me. As long as I stayed out of my mother's line of sight, I was invisible in the house. I never got involved in the fights and sparring the boys engaged in every day. I would leave my bedroom window slightly open so I could sneak into my room without going through the back door into the kitchen, where my mother seemed to live. I could rely on my oldest brother to poke his head into my room and tell me it was time for me to lay the table for dinner, a chore reserved for me only. Clearing the table and doing the dishes after were also considered female chores. More often than not, either my oldest brother or my father would help me with the dishes. Talking was not permitted at the table unless one of our parents asked us a specific question and, as stated, it was clearly felt that we children would have nothing to say worth hearing.

In fact, listening was openly discouraged at home. If ever I came upon my mother speaking to another member of the family or a visiting friend and paused, she would immediately round on me, accusing me of "earwigging." I would be told to hurry up and leave the room straightaway; banished without even being given the chance to say hello.

As an inquisitive child, and one who already instinctively understood the value of the story, and in hearing what others had to say, this had the opposite effect on me. I wanted to know what it was adults talked about, wanted to know everything. I sensed that there were things I wasn't meant to hear, and this made me even more determined to find them out. I knew so little about my own family, yet it was clear there were a lot of secrets being whispered.

The day I heard my mother and grandmother talking about the death of my friend's father shocked me.

My friend hadn't been at school for two days, but no reason had been given. I never understood why I couldn't be told this so I could comfort her. It was weeks before she returned to school and she told me she had had to stay at home and help with her younger siblings because her mother wouldn't come out of her bedroom. Her days at school became fewer and fewer. When I asked my mother why she thought my friend wasn't coming to school, she told me there were more important things to do than go to school when people needed looking after and it was none of my business. She never did mention the death of my friend's father directly to me.

One day, it occurred to me that it was the women in my family—my mother, grandmother, aunts—who never told me anything, never listened to anything I had to say. Not as chatty as my great-grandfather, my father was, however, a very good listener to me, his only daughter. If I got him alone, in a good mood, at the end of the day—and particularly if my mother wasn't around—we would talk.

He seemed to need to apologize for the way my mother treated me, tried to explain it away as her having to work so hard raising us children and her life wasn't what she would want for me. This never made sense to me. Like Gramps, my father was a gentle, quietly spoken man, who I never heard raise his voice. When he could, on weekends or school holidays, he would make an effort to spend time with my older brother and me, taking us for walks through the paddocks and telling us little bits about his life back in Scotland. He had strong morals and a sense of right and wrong. He hated gossip. I was so proud of my father one day when, peering around the corner into the kitchen where my mother and grandmother sat gossiping, I watched him walk into the room, pour himself a glass of milk, and stand there drinking it while the two women ignored his presence.

He was only there a minute or two, but clearly didn't like what he was hearing. I heard him tell my grandmother he had heard enough malicious talk and it was time for her to leave. Taking offense at this, my grandmother approached him, yelling abuse, accusing him of being an outsider who didn't belong there. He told her quietly to go home. From the bench, my grandmother picked up a dinner plate and smashed it over his head. He simply said, "It is definitely time for you to leave."

My mother followed her mother outside, apologizing and saying he didn't mean anything. I stepped into the room and asked my father if he was all right.

He gave me the biggest smile, said he was fine and that she—my grandmother—had probably been wanting to do that for years. Together, we cleaned up the broken plate.

He was an outsider, he told me. Nobody in the family listened to him or sought his counsel. My mother's family had lived in the village and surrounding area for five generations. My father had been born in Scotland and moved to New Zealand as an adult, his family unknown to the locals. Born into a large family, one of the youngest of sixteen children, he had studied medicine for four years before abandoning his passion to be a doctor and joining the British Army as a medic in the war. He said virtually nothing to me about his military service, only that he couldn't go back to the life he had prior to signing up and so he fled to New Zealand. Working the land was the only thing that gave him pleasure. As such, I think he felt he was never fully accepted into the family, into the community. It didn't seem to bother him.

I regret most sincerely that I didn't ask him very much about his family. I know bits and pieces, but not a lot really. I hadn't learned that if you want to know something you must first ask, or at least, at that time, what I *had* learned was that I absolutely was not to ask, ever. I waited for him to tell me, in the way that Gramps did. Or perhaps I had been discouraged so often from asking questions by my mother and her family that I thought I would get the same response from my father. And perhaps he didn't tell me because he was so used to the family around him having little interest in the stories that he might have chosen to tell. I regret deeply that I did not make more effort to know my father better, have him tell me stories of his past, hopes, and dreams. He knew most days I spent time with Gramps, often asking, "How was the old man today?" and listening to me relay in detail what I had listened to. He knew how much I loved hearing stories, even the same story over and over, yet he never offered to do the same as Gramps. He also knew I never shared my time with Gramps with my mother. To her I was simply doing my duty being with him—how wrong she was!

When later in life I found myself working in the social work department of a large hospital, it seemed so easy to listen to patients, their families, and their carers. I often thought of Gramps and how listening to him had trained me to listen and hear what was being said to me. Only by listening could I respond and try to help. Just having someone listen can often be enough, without any further intervention. I saw enough in Gramps's eyes to know for certain that he found comfort in talking to me, a peace within himself that he was at long last sharing his experiences and being heard.

Given what has transpired in my meeting and talking with Holocaust survivors, all well into their senior years, only now do I reflect back on my time listening to my great-grandfather and connect the dots—his age, his advancing years, and his need to talk to someone who would listen. Perhaps I was just the right person, at the right time in his life. By the time my father reached the same age, I was married, with young children, living in a different country. Begs the question, did he find someone, a carer at the facility where he lived his final year, to talk to?

Because of the success of my novels *The Tattooist of Auschwitz* and *Cilka's Journey*, and the appalling period of history to which they relate, I have had the privilege of meeting many people who shared the experiences of Lale, Gita, and Cilka. All over the world, in many countries and in many different venues and events, Holocaust survivors come to hear me speak and to spend time—a few minutes, often longer—sharing stories from their lives. At the end of these events I often find myself hearing the most amazing stories, of survival, of love—of hope. I also receive messages and letters from people from all over the world who, moved by the novels, reach out to share their own experience with me. What has surprised and touched me is the number of people who have reached out to me with a story that is not connected to the Holocaust. Other survivors of illness, of tragic deaths in their families, of more recent conflicts. They all have one thing in common: they have read Lale and Gita's story and taken hope from it. Hope that they too can have a good life. Hope that their children and grandchildren will have good lives because of, or despite, their own suffering.

The capacity of older men and women to briefly and succinctly tell me a story of overwhelming emotion and pain, ending with, "But I've had a good life," always leaves me in awe of just how inspirational and uplifting these "ordinary" people are. That they have lived through our history—they are our *living* history— deserves recognition. They don't seek anything in return. Just someone to listen to them, acknowledge their past, validate the choices they made to be here today. Hearing those stories has been a gift to me, an enormous privilege. Being able to turn some of them into works of fiction has changed my life utterly. And I do believe that it all stems from knowing how to listen.

One evening in early 2020, I found myself sitting in the lounge room of a ninety-two-year-old woman in Israel, a survivor who knew Lale and Gita in Auschwitz. How I got to be there is a story I'll come back to later in this book. As we sat, her daughter read out loud, translating from Hebrew to English for me, the testimony of her deceased aunt, this old woman's sister. This old woman is one of the three sisters whose story I tell in my novel *Three Sisters*. I often think of the last words written in that testimony, which is in the family's private ownership. Those final words are: *Do Not Judge Us*.

Too often, people have voiced criticism to me of the choices Lale made in surviving the Holocaust. Sure, he bent the rules, sure he survived where so many didn't. That is the guilt of all Holocaust survivors. Too often, I am forced to bite my tongue, acknowledge they are entitled to their own opinion, inwardly screaming the words, *you do not get to judge. You weren't there, you cannot know, you cannot imagine even if you think you can, you cannot tell me the choices you would have made under the same circumstances.* I hasten to add not one of those critical of Lale, Gita, and Cilka's choices was there in the camps. And so often it wasn't even a decision or choice—it just happened that they were the lucky ones to whom an opportunity presented itself, on whom a random and very rare act of kindness was bestowed.

In our modern, youth-obsessed culture, when you reach a certain age, it seems, you become invisible, unless you are a celebrity—and famous women are so often criticized and held up for ridicule. Your grandparent, your elderly neighbor, the stranger you bump into on the street because you didn't see them, all have stories and wisdom, which, if only we took the time to listen, might just enrich our lives beyond measure. We—and I now include myself in the ranks of the "invisible"—do not want to tell you how you should live your life. We do not want to warn you about our mistakes in life, so you don't make the same ones. Quite the opposite. You need to make your own mistakes—that's how you learn. But if you take the time to listen to the life journeys and experiences of those near to you, you might just discover how to learn more quickly from your own mistakes. You might learn something about those around you that seems very relevant, similar, to a situation you now find yourself in. Listening, *really listening* to people, is richly rewarding. This, I know without doubt.

A pandemic is sweeping the world. A pandemic

which is killing elderly people in far higher numbers than the young. We are asked to social distance and quarantine as a mark of respect for the elderly family and friends we all have, to keep them safe. A sore throat or a sniffle for a young person can be deadly to an older one. Surely the moral wealth of a country should be measured by how it treats the very people who have built the communities around them. It is humbling to read of the large number of people across all countries and communities who have volunteered to assist those who are isolated and without means to support and shop for themselves. This includes the group identified as "senior citizens." I have heard reports of so much kindness that elderly family members have asked their caring family and friends to slow down—there is only so much they can eat!

Being compassionate and giving to the elderly differs between communities and cultures. While I read to my great-grandmother, sat and listened to my great-grandfather, it was my mother who made sure they had the best meals she was capable of preparing each day. With five children and often farm laborers to feed too, she lived by the motto that first you feed the animals, the elderly, the babies, and then the rest. It always amused me that she put the animals before any humans.

It wasn't just because Gramps was our family elder that he was loved and respected. We all knew of his experience as a young man going off to war. All family members who fought, many making the ultimate sacrifice with their lives, were honored and respected in my family. None more so than him.

Gramps traveled from New Zealand to South Africa to fight in what is known as the Boer War (1899–1902). It was effectively a war of independence—the "Boer" states, which are now modern South Africa, seeking to throw off the British Empire. As with so many conflicts, young men in the colonies were expected to sign up and fight alongside the British Army. Gramps shouldn't have been there. He was too young. His older brother wanted to enlist, and their mother asked Gramps to ride (on horseback) from their home to Auckland, a journey of some two hundred kilometers, to keep him company. It took them three days, two nights, sleeping in farmers' barns along the way. They would be fed and sent on their way the next morning.

The criteria for being signed up by the British (New Zealand didn't have its own Army at this time) was the ability to ride confidently. My great-grandfather watched his brother gallop the required distance. Then a nearby officer indicated for him to do the same, so he did—he rode better than his sibling. They asked him to sign on the dotted line. He did; he had just signed up to go to war. A month later, the two brothers rode back to Auckland and together with their own horses (yes, it was BYO horse!), they sailed to South Africa. My great-grandfather was just sixteen. His mother had begged him not to go. *It was a mistake; he was too young.* His father apparently told her to "Let the boy make his own choice." Gramps told me there was no way he was letting his brother, James, have all the fun. Of course, that isn't what he meant—he did not want him to be alone, with no family, so far from home. He was leaving behind four sisters and a brother, thirteen years younger, just a toddler.

Not long after Gramps arrived in South Africa, he lined up for inspection by Field Marshal Horatio Herbert Kitchener. When asked his age, he admitted to being only sixteen. Kitchener had him taken out of combat and gave him a role as his "boy," doing odd jobs for him and accompanying him wherever he went. Kitchener wrote home to Gramps's mother, telling her he would take care of her son and return him home safe and sound. My great-great-grandmother received two letters from the Field Marshal, which are now in a local museum. I held these letters on several occasions, reading the elegant handwriting, knowing they were treasured family possessions. Several years later, when I visited the museum, my chest swelled with pride as I saw the collection of artifacts and these letters, all with little cards beside them indicating they were on loan from my family. And Kitchener returned her son home to her, safe and sound. His older brother also returned to New Zealand.

These are the stories Gramps spent those afternoons on the back veranda telling me. How, as a sixteen-year-old boy, he traveled with Field Marshal Kitchener all over South Africa. How he spent time among African tribes. He told me tales of campaigns that were waged, how he knew a lot in advance because he worked so closely with Kitchener. Those precious artifacts that he brought back with him, that he would let me hold as he explained how he came about them, also now reside in a museum. It would be easy to make disparaging remarks about Kitchener and his role in South Africa. Many others have done so. I remain grateful that through his actions in looking after my great-grandfather, I was born and have lived this wonderful, rich, rewarding life. Sometimes it's as simple as that, isn't it? Politics and history aside, it is small acts of humanity that echo down through generations.

I knew my great-grandfather never spoke openly about this time to anyone else, that what he told me was our secret and ours alone, not to be repeated to anyone. He would tell me how my great-grandmother didn't want him talking about it. Sound familiar? I never heard him talking about his life to any other member of my family, either individually or at a family gathering. More often than not, I was aware of how acutely sad he sounded when he told me of the brutality of war he had witnessed, particularly when it related to the African peoples.

Many times, I overheard the adult family members around me commenting on how grumpy or withdrawn he was. It appeared to me that he was largely ignored by them, all the attention going to my great-grandmother. While he was seldom physically affectionate toward me, or anyone else for that matter, each time I saw him—which was every day for many years—he greeted me with a warm smile, a pat on the arm, or if other family were around, a wink. All my life I have known that for this one person, this one man, I was someone special. I think I helped him, because I listened, and he was enormously important to me as a child. In a family devoid of emotional and physical affection, he was a great comfort to me at a time when I most needed it.

In April 1971 I left my small town in New Zealand to find my way in the big city of Melbourne, Australia. Before going to the airport, I visited my great-grandfather in Ranfurly Veterans Home and Hospital in Auckland, where he had lived for a short period. We sat on the veranda overlooking a garden, not too dissimilar to the one we sat on together when I was a child. This time I did most of the talking as I told him of my need to spread my wings. He told me it was the best thing I could do, to leave the town I had grown up in, where everyone knew me, to find my own place in this world. He died five months later on September 29. I did not return for his funeral. I didn't need to. He knew how I felt about him. I preferred to grieve alone.

My own grandchildren are very young. All they need to hear from their grandma now is how much she loves them, loves being with them, and wants to listen to them. They are great little storytellers already. A simple event at day care or school is told in detail, often accompanied by dramatic gestures. I listen intently, loving the expression and joy the retelling brings to little faces.

I hope as they grow older, I can become for each of them that person my great-grandfather was to me. Someone prepared to listen, no matter what, to whatever they have to say. Its importance does not matter, what matters is giving them the space to be heard. And perhaps, if they listen to me, I'll be able to share with them some of the stories I have heard along my life journey. Perhaps one day I'll tell them about Gramps.

If there is a family member or friend you know who has something they treasure, small or large, valuable or not, ask them what it means to them. Give them the opportunity to share with you their connection to that object. It may have monetary value, it may be something as simple as a marble, but it is priceless to the owner. Whatever it is, there will be a story connected to it. Below are some ideas around getting our elders to unlock their past.

Practical Tips for How to Listen to Our Elders

Who doesn't recognize the regret after a beloved elderly friend or relative dies: "Oh, if only I'd asked them about . . . ?" Yet in the midst of our busy lives it often seems hard to find the time to sit down and listen to stories we might have heard a dozen times before. My advice to you is to set aside that time, for once the opportunity has gone, it is gone forever.

Simple Questions

With age, even among those who are suffering from Alzheimer's or other diseases of dementia, early memories often become sharper. Your parents or grandparents will probably remember their early childhood or schooldays with a clarity they could not during their busy working lives. You can, if you know them well, ask about their favorite toys, their first day at school, perhaps the very first thing they can recall. These memories are generally safe places to start their journey back into the past, but specific questions, often based on something you are doing together, can also be a useful way of beginning a conversation. As you share a cup of tea and a slice of cake, for instance, try asking:

"What was your favorite food as a child?"

"Who did the cooking in the family?"

"When and where did you have your meals?"

"Did you always sit in the same place around the table?"

"Did you have your own special mug or plate?"

Direct questions like these, arising naturally from a shared experience (in this case, the cup of tea and cake) and requiring simple, factual answers, can lead someone to reveal how they felt about their family and home and their place in it. Follow the answers, prompt gently for more details, and you may find a new willingness to share insights into their lives.

It takes time—as I know from my own experiences with Lale—to build up trust between an older and a younger person, but if you start slowly with those sort of deceptively simple questions outlined, you will find that you have a strong basis for moving the conversation on. You can always use those basic questions as a safe jumping-off point for deeper reflection:

> "We were talking last time about how much you loved your mother's teacakes. Can you remember her making them? Did she let you help? How did you feel when she put them on the plate in front of you?"

What you are really opening up here is a conversation about the sort of childhood your elder had, but because you are asking something quite specific it is much less threatening and abstract than addressing the question directly. The answer may lead on to further reflections on their life as a child, building up a circle of trust and interest that will pay huge dividends. Seeing involuntary smiles, spontaneous giggles, as a memory is brought to mind and shared, is a beautiful thing.

Using Objects
A cup of tea (or in my case with Lale, a terrible cup of coffee!) is a comforting domestic ritual.

But after you've poured, sipped, and refilled, unless your elder is in full reminiscence mode, there's a limit to the opportunity it offers for the safe sharing of the past. If you feel you have hit a brick wall and really can't face drinking another cup, I'd recommend encouraging the conversation by introducing a physical object.

As I have already said, on my visits to Gramps, he would often have something ready to show me—the letters Kitchener wrote to his parents, the *toki*, his medals. He would pass these precious objects to me and as I turned them over and over in my hands, examining them from all angles, he would explain the background and tell me the story that lay behind each of them. Instinctively, I kept my focus on the object itself, rather than making eye contact with Gramps, and I think this gave him the space to concentrate and reminisce more freely without having to watch for my reactions to what he was saying. It is not necessary to maintain eye contact all the time when talking to someone who is remembering their past—in fact, I would say avoid it, let their eyes wander off. They possibly won't be looking at you, they will have gone back to the memory, time, and place. Leave them there for as long as they want.

My friend Jenny described visiting her elderly mother-in-law to help her pack up and move from the home she had lived in for over sixty years. As the two women packed and sorted every piece of furniture, every picture, every ornament, Jenny's mother-in-law described each thing in loving detail—where and when she had bought it, or who had given it to her, and how important it was to her. Jenny described her mother-in-law as a very private person, not normally willing to divulge details of her personal life, but through this shared practical task and using the objects they were packing together, she was able to find a way of passing on important family history.

If you are visiting an elder regularly, why not take along something to help spur a memory? Perhaps they have mentioned a vacation they once took—bring a map or find some photographs of the place and look at them together. Maybe they sit in a favorite old chair—where did they buy it? How did it arrive in their sitting room? There will probably be photographs on display. Choose one and ask if you can look at it more closely, and if you don't know, find out who is in the picture and when and where the photos were taken. Ornaments or other pictures can also unlock memories and encourage stories. Take care when you handle these objects: the fact that they are on display, or have been kept carefully for so many years, indicates how precious they are—not necessarily in value, but for what they represent.

Reflection

By now, you should have established a level of trust and a bridge across the different generations. Your elder may have shared anecdotes from their own life and perhaps—if they are family members—memories of your own childhood. You will be seeing this elderly person in a new light as a vigorous, independent person with a past life and experiences they want to share. Once you feel you have earned the right to go a little deeper into their past, you might like to invite them to reflect on some of the lessons they have learned over the years.

Again, I always prefer not to address this directly. In my experience, explicitly asking for tips on life usually results in unwanted practical advice (although I must admit I've often given it myself and it's *not wrong*): "Always polish your shoes," "Treat others as you would wish to be treated yourself," "Wear clean underwear in case you get hit by a bus." What I'm after— and what I hope you're after, if you're reading this book—is something a bit more reflective. Here's one way to go about it . . .

Why not ask your elder what they would tell their younger selves if they were sitting there in front of them? If they could meet that probably nervous, uncertain, young person, what sort of reassurance and guidance would they offer? What would they tell them to avoid, what would they tell them to embrace, and what would they tell them they would be most proud of? It might help to position an empty chair close by and in-vite your elder to pretend their younger self is sitting right there, so that you both turn your gaze away and focus on the chair to avoid the intensity of looking at each other. You might ask what they are wearing, whether or not they are likely to be listening, even how they are sitting physically in the chair. Take your time establishing an authentic connection with this younger self and take it slowly—this is an exercise that can pack a real emotional punch and offer you, the listener, a life lesson you won't forget.

I should say up front that I never did this exercise with Lale. His need to tell his story—however painful it was—was too urgent for me to do anything but listen, build trust, and then follow where he led me, gently probing for detail where I felt I could or should. Although most elders are not Holocaust survivors, many will need some persuasion to share their own stories and some may not feel that they have anything exceptional to pass on. But I disagree: each of us has lived a unique life, we all have something to say that is worth listening to. I hope that you will feel encouraged to try some of these ways of opening up a conversation with an elderly person—I can guarantee that it will be time well spent.

2

Listening to Lale

"If you wake up in the morning, then it's a good day." Lale Sokolov

In December 2003, I caught up with a friend I hadn't seen for a few months. Over coffee and a chat, she casually said to me, "You're interested in writing screenplays, aren't you? I have a friend whose mother has just died. His father, aged eighty-seven, has asked him to find someone he can tell a story to—that person can't be Jewish. You're not Jewish, would you like to meet him?" I asked her if she knew what the story was about and she said no, not really. Intrigued,

I said yes. A week later, on a sunny, Southern Hemisphere summer Sunday afternoon, I left home to meet Lale Sokolov.

Happy Hanukkah. *Haapppy Hanukkah!* I rehearse this foreign phrase while driving to my meeting. Hanukkah I know vaguely to be the Jewish festival of lights. Through suburbs, their streets festooned with Christmas decorations, I ponder what my opening line should be. Can my Kiwi accent pull off a heartfelt "Happy Hanukkah" without sounding silly? Oh, but wait . . . The man I'm meeting has recently lost his wife. Maybe using a phrase which includes the word "happy" is inappropriate. My mood changes. No longer do the sparkling wreaths, sleigh bells, and jolly santas surrounding me make me smile. My approaching destination now fills me with apprehension.

The door opens, revealing a small, thin, elderly gentleman. Two dogs, one on each side, form a guard. One of the dogs is no bigger than my cat; the other is the size of a small pony, but nowhere near as friendly-looking.

"I am Lale, these are my kiddos, Tootsie and Bam Bam."

This seems to serve sufficiently as an introduction as the next word is "Come," which comes out not so much as an invitation as an order. They all turn abruptly and shuffle in single file down the corridor. After shutting the door, I follow. I've not been given a chance for any greeting and I've not worked out which name belongs to which kiddo.

The convoy enters an immaculate room, which is a shrine to the 1960s. It stops at a superbly polished large dining table.

"Sit."

This is a directive, with a chosen chair at the table pointed out to me. I sit. Satisfied, Lale and the kiddos shuffle off into an adjacent room. I'm left to check out my surroundings, the influence of a house-proud woman evident throughout. Oversized blooms on the large scatter rugs, the walls adorned with prints and family photos, a nearby sideboard filled with exquisite crystal, above which hangs a painting that draws me to it: a Gypsy woman kneeling on a pink rug laid out on dirt, a red flower tucked behind her left ear, a large hoop dangling from her right ear, luxurious black hair falling in waves to her shoulders. A three-strand necklace encircles her neck, her lips are soft and pink, and dark piercing eyes stare straight ahead as if looking into a camera lens. She is wearing a bottle-green full skirt with an off-white blouse, the sleeves ballooning above her elbows. Her bag and scarf lie partially obscured behind her. The toes of a bare foot poke from under her skirt. Four playing cards are spread out in front of her. She is pointing to one: it appears to be the Ace of Hearts.

A few minutes later, Lale and the kiddos triumphantly reappear. A cup and saucer, a side plate with six wafer cookies neatly presented on it are placed before me. Lale sits to my right, the kiddos stand guard either side.

"Have you had these before?" he asks, indicating the cookies.

"Yes, wafer biscuits are one of the few things you can still get that I remember from my childhood."

"But I bet they weren't these biscuits . . ."

Once again, I'm left alone as the three of them shuffle off once more to the kitchen. They all reappear, and a cookie packet is placed before me. The comings and goings are starting to unsettle me and I'm unsure what to say in case they all disappear again.

"There, have you had these before?" he repeats.

Sitting, the kiddos now lie down, one either side of him, their eyes still firmly on me.

"No, I'm pretty sure I've not had this brand before."

"Didn't think so. They're from Israel, see. You can't read that, can you?"

I turn the packet over, looking at the foreign writing.

"I'm guessing that's Hebrew writing, so no, I can't read it, but I can tell you they're bloody good biscuits!"

The first hint of a smile.

"How quick can you write?"

"I can't answer that question, it depends on what I'm writing."

"Well, you better be quick because I don't have much time."

First hint of panic. I had deliberately chosen not to bring any writing material with me, I just wanted to listen to the story I had been requested to hear and consider writing about. Glancing at my watch, I ask him: "I'm sorry, how much time do you have?"

"Not much."

"Do you have to be somewhere else?"

"Yes, I need to be with my Gita."

I try to make eye contact with this frail eighty-seven-year-old man who has just uttered his recently deceased wife's name. His head remains bowed.

"Mr. Sokolov, I don't want to upset you. If you don't want to talk to me, that's OK, you make good coffee and I'm really enjoying your biscuits."

But I was lying to him—this was the first of what would be many, many bad cups of coffee Lale would make for me.

"You never met Gita, did you?"

"No."

"Would you like to see her picture?"

Before I can answer, he and his companions are on their feet again, heading toward a nearby cabinet, housing a large television and a photo of Gita and Lale.

Handing me the photo, he said: "She was the most beautiful girl I'd ever seen. I held her hand and looked into her frightened eyes and I tattooed numbers on her arm. Did you know that? Did you know I was the Tattooist in Auschwitz?"

Riveted by the photo of the smiling, seventy-something Gita, sat next to this beautiful man, his arm around her, I am stunned, silent, not yet taking in what he is telling me.

The photo is put back in its place, positioned just so. I notice both it and the television are lined up for perfect viewing from a nearby recliner chair.

"Since you've come here, I should tell you my story, no?"

"Only if you want to."

I look down at his companions, who now look as though they may be asleep.

"I was a good-looking guy back then." Riffling through his wallet, he pulls out an aging passport photo and hands it to me. A handsome, smiling twenty-four-year-old Ludwig Eisenberg looks back at me—he later told me how he changed his name to Sokolov after the war, in order to sound "Russian," and I guess also to conceal that he was Jewish. No, more than handsome, in the one photo I see arrogance, self-assuredness; he is cheeky, suave, a man confident of who he is and his place in the world.

"I was a mumma's boy. I've always known it, never denied it."

"And . . ."

"And what?"

For the next two hours I sat listening as Lale spoke, recounting snippets of stories, fragmented, often told at bullet pace with limited coherency and no flow or connection linking them. He slipped out of English into what I guessed was Slovakian, sometimes German, and occasionally some Russian and Polish. The kiddos hadn't moved but eventually I sensed that Lale was getting restless, tired. When he said he had been the *Tätowierer* in Auschwitz, I interrupted to ask what he meant. He looked at me as if I was stupid. I wasn't sure if it was because I had interrupted him, or I should have known what he was referring to.

"Tattooist, I was the tattooist in Auschwitz-Birkenau—I made the numbers," he explained patiently. "I made *her* number. I held her hand while I made her number and I looked into her eyes." He didn't need to say who he was talking about. "I knew then, I knew in that second, that I could never love another."

The chills I get writing this fifteen years later were the same as when I first heard Lale say those words: "I could never love another."

The photo of him and Gita, which had been placed on the table between us, Gita having joined the conversation, was now clutched to his chest. I could hear his broken heart pounding. I could feel my own quicken as his grief and pain reached across the table and hit me.

I reached out and gently placed my hand on his arm. His shirt sleeve slid down, partially revealing his own numbers. I fixated on them. He noticed. As

I removed my hand, he pulled his sleeve up and held out his left arm proudly in front of me.

"32407," he said. The fading blue-green numbers held my attention.

"Who?" I whispered. "Who tattooed you, do you know?"

"Sure, I know. It was Pepan. Pepan gave me my number."

A short while later, I asked Lale if he followed tennis. I felt I needed to end his talking about a dark, painful period of his life. I knew enough about talking to people in tragic and traumatic times to switch them from the topic they were talking about—break the spell that had enclosed us both. If *I* was feeling distressed hearing his half-told stories, how was *he* feeling?

Yes, he loved tennis. And football, and basketball, and athletics, he told me.

"What about cricket?" I asked. "It's cricket season."

Nope, he was not a fan of cricket. Couldn't see the point of a game that could be played for five days and still not have a winner.

Eventually I sensed that it was time to leave: "Can I come back and see you next week?" I asked.

"I need to ask you something before I answer. How much do you know about the Holocaust?"

I hung my head in shame. "I'm so sorry," I said, "my small-town New Zealand education all those years ago taught me very little and I'm embarrassed to tell you I have not added very much knowledge since then."

"Perfect," he said. "You will be perfect."

"I need to ask *you* something, Mr. Sokolov. Why do you want to talk to someone who is not Jewish?"

"Simple. I want to talk to someone who has no connection to the Holocaust."

"Why?"

"I don't believe there is a Jewish person alive, anywhere, who is not affected by the Holocaust, either personally or through family or friends. They will have baggage and will not be able to write my story."

"You do know I haven't written a book before? I have studied and written a few screenplays, none of which have gotten anywhere."

I needed to confess to my nonexistent writing accomplishments. Being a lover of film, I naively thought if I spent my weekends going to screenwriting classes and tutorials, reading movie scripts and studying the finished films, I could write a screenplay. I had several plots in mind and saw all my stories visually as they played out in my head. Confidence in one's ability to accomplish something should never be underestimated. You are not a failure because you tried something and it didn't come off, you just try harder the next time. Or so I had been telling myself. I had only written one screenplay.

"You can write, right?" Lale asked.

"I think so."

"Then write my story."

"There is one thing I think you should know about me."

At this, he looked for the first time directly at me.

"I need to tell you my mother's maiden name. It was Schwartfeger."

"Ah, you German," he said in his most animated voice that day.

"No, I'm a Kiwi. I'm from New Zealand, five generations of my family were born there."

"No matter, we can't choose our parents, can we?"

Hearing this, we shared our first smile.

"Tuesday, come on Tuesday," he said.

"Umm, I work Monday to Friday."

"What time do you finish?"

"Five o'clock."

"Well then, I'll see you after that."

I didn't notice the street decorations as I drove

home, my brain scrambled with pictures of horror and love, evil and courage.

"How was it?" my family asked when I returned home.

"I've just spent time with living history," was my only response. Pressured to say more, I couldn't or wouldn't. For now, I needed to be left alone with my thoughts as I tried to interpret what I had been told, where it sat with my limited knowledge of the Holocaust and how significant this man's story was—I had no idea.

I returned on Tuesday after work and again on Thursday and Sunday afternoons. We sat at his dining table, his bad coffee and yummy wafer cookies between us. He talked, I listened. Lale seldom made eye contact. He talked to the table, to the wall, to one of his kiddos as he leaned down and often scratched one or other of them behind the ear. Occasionally, one of them fetched a tennis ball and brought it to him. He would throw it over his shoulder and the two dogs chased and fought for it—Tootsie always won, but Bam Bam never stopped trying.

At no time did I attempt to write down anything Lale was saying in front of him. I toyed with asking him if I could record him but never did. The few times I interrupted him to ask a question, he got flustered and lost his thread, unable to continue the story he was relating. But it didn't matter. Sitting with him and the kiddos, listening to what was at times the ramblings of an elderly gentleman, was spellbinding. Was it the delightful Eastern European accent? Was it the charm this rascal had lived his life dispensing? Or, was it the twisted, convoluted story I was starting to make sense of, the significance and importance of which was beginning to dawn on me? It was all of these things and more.

I would race home, ignore the questions and demands of my husband and three young adult children, go directly to my computer, and try to remember all I had heard, the names, times, and places. My spelling of the names, particularly the ranks of the SS officers he referred to, was comical, looking back. I also had a separate spreadsheet, where I recorded the date and time, how I thought Lale was emotionally that day and how I felt, during and after being with him.

For several weeks I visited him two or three times a week. He and the kiddos always greeted me at the door, with Lale's opening words . . .

"Have you finished my book yet? You know I want to be with Gita."

I would respond with, "No, I haven't and remember, Lale, I'm writing a screenplay, not a book."

He'd ignore this as he held the door open for me to enter, then waited for me to take my seat at the table before he and the kiddos disappeared into the kitchen, returning with the "coffee" and cookies.

Lale was still grieving terribly. Listening to his stories was one thing, watching him as he told them quite another. It was clear to me he was conflicted: he wanted to join Gita, but he also wanted their story told and there was still so much to tell. Some days his grief and depression hung over him like a cloud fit to burst. On these days I noticed that Tootsie and Bam Bam lay quietly at their master's feet. I would take my cue from their behavior as to his mood. On other days he was animated, so alive talking about "his Gita." I remain eternally grateful to Tootsie and Bam Bam for their doggy intuition and unconditional love for Lale that not only helped him but helped me become part of their tight group. I had my own dog (Lucy) and knew and believed wholeheartedly in the strength and comfort a wet nose and puppy-dog eyes can give.

Lale was getting used to me. He was warm, welcoming, could easily engage in telling me about his life before Auschwitz, mixing it in with his life with

Gita in Australia. Facts, clinical descriptions, wonderful, but all too often he started saying something, paused, then switched to something else. Every time he touched the raw emotion he had lived with for his nearly-ninety years, through one of the darkest, most evil periods of history, he pulled back from it.

One Sunday afternoon, I asked him what he was having for dinner. He had some leftover soup, he told me. On an impulse, I invited him to come and have dinner with my family and me and he accepted without hesitation, his face lighting up. Quickly feeding the doggies when I gently pointed out to him that my dog would not welcome extra four-legged friends to dinner, he let me drive him to my home.

My eighteen-year-old daughter was not expecting to have her hand kissed when she extended it to Lale on meeting him. My husband and two sons were immediately enchanted with him and conversation came easily. When my husband and I went into the kitchen to prepare dinner, the children remained in the lounge room with Lale. A short while later, I heard a sound I had not heard before and it made me stop what I was doing in wonder and delight: Lale was laughing. I poked my head around the door and there he was, sitting on a sofa with my daughter, making her laugh out loud, engaged in what I described later as good old-fashioned flirtation.

The evening was wonderful. We sat around our dining table, eating and talking for hours. Lale held everyone captive, but not with stories of the Holocaust. For the first time I was hearing about his life growing up before he was sent to Auschwitz; his life in Bratislava after liberation and his life with Gita living in Australia.

Was I seeing a new Lale, or was this the Lale of old? The grieving elderly gentleman who had a story of such horror and evil was changing before my eyes. I started to realize how it was he had survived. He was full of charisma, charming not only my daughter but my husband and sons too. It was obvious they had warmed to him immediately, were captivated by his courage and intelligence on hearing his stories.

Lale insisted my daughter and I stay seated when it was time to clean up; he would help the other men do the dishes. Out in the kitchen I overheard him asking the men in my family about me and was mortified at some of the things they said. My sons told him I wasn't a great cook, that their father was more creative in meal preparation. My husband told him how I was the untidy one and it was he who did most of the housework. OK, so there's a grain of truth in what they said. What I remember most vividly about that first visit to my home was Lale's laughter. It was the first time I had heard him laugh and from then on he would laugh and giggle every time we met, over the smallest, silliest things.

On the drive home I commented on his "flirting" with my daughter. His first response was, "She's a very pretty girl!" After a few moments of silence, he added, "She's the same age Gita was when I met her." It now made sense. Something about my daughter reminded Lale so powerfully of Gita and their first years together.

Introducing Lale to my family, letting him see who I was, having him listen to my family, enjoy jokes at my expense, have them tell him stories about me, gave him the connection to me that he needed to trust me a little bit more. That trust went to another level a few days later when Tootsie came to the table where we were sitting. As usual, she had a tennis ball in her mouth, but this time she growled when Lale tried to take it from her.

"Naughty Tootsie, give me the ball," he said, giving her a small tap on her head.

She growled again. We were both shocked. Tootsie and Bam Bam were the perfect companions, only ever barking when the postman on his scooter stopped below Lale's apartment to deliver mail.

Tootsie turned away from Lale, took the one step to get closer to me, and rested her head on my knee, the ball balanced between her teeth, her big eyes meeting mine. Cautiously, I reached down and put my hand in her mouth, around the tennis ball. She released it and stepped away. When I threw it over my shoulder, the kiddos scampered to be the one to retrieve it. Lale and I watched them before he turned to me.

"My kiddos like you, I like you, you can tell my story," he said finally.

This small, inconsequential event was like hitting a switch with Lale. The next time I visited him, he greeted me with, "Have you finished my book yet?" This time, there wasn't the follow-up, "I have to be with Gita." Now he was fully engrossed in wanting to have his story told.

The emotional outpouring when talking about Gita, his mother and father and his sister Goldie, the only member of his family to survive, was overwhelming. Lale's retelling of his time in Auschwitz-

Birkenau left me angry and filled with rage, but I noticed a further change in his behavior. As he began to speak more emotionally of his past, a weight seemed to lift from him and he appeared happier.

Our relationship moved from subject and writer to one of friendship. He still did the majority of the talking; I was there to listen. Drawing these stories and their attendant memories from him was an enormous task. By now I was doing a lot of background reading, confirming names of places and people and corroborating the details of Lale's time in Auschwitz-Birkenau. I was constantly aware of the way memory and history sometimes waltz in step and sometimes strain and part. Lale's memory seemed clear and precise and chimed with my research. Was this a comfort to me? No, it made his memories all the more horrific; there was very little parting of memory and history for this beautiful old man, too often they waltzed perfectly in step. As I learned more about what Gita's life in the camp was like from other survivors Lale introduced me to, I understood why he wanted to talk about their time together and not face what she endured when not with him.

After several months, Lale began to ask me to accompany him to social events and to visit friends.

The first time I entered a function with him, I was confronted by a room with men standing on one side, women on the other. We stood at the entrance as Lale was greeted warmly by everyone there, so happy to see their friend again. He pointed to me and loudly exclaimed, "She my girlfriend! Ladies, look after her—I will pick her up on the way out." The charm and wit this delightful man had dispensed all his life was back and on display for all.

Did I mind being sent to spend time with the "ladies"? Not at all. Now I got to listen to a wonderful group of female survivors, all eager to share not only stories of their survival but tales of the decades spent with Lale and Gita in the Jewish community in Melbourne. How privileged was I?

The next day, I reflected on this, the first of many such experiences. So little was asked of and about me, everyone wanted to talk and have my attention. Listening as excited women talked over each other, finished each other's sentences, argued and contradicted each other was wonderful. Whenever I did speak, it was to ask a question, often about Lale or Gita, or to get more detail about a story, a small vignette told.

I was also privileged to meet friends of the couple

on one-to-one occasions. Listening to Lale and one of his friends, a fellow survivor, talk, laugh, rib each other about their experiences was incredibly humbling. To be welcomed into his circle, where his friends opened up to me, appreciating the role I had in his life, was wonderful. His friend, Tuli, had only been seventeen when taken from his hometown of Bardejov in Slovakia. "A skinny little kid—the wind could blow me over," was how he described himself to me. Like Lale, he suffered sickness along with the starvation and degradation. He was subsequently moved from Auschwitz-Birkenau to another camp to work, which he credits with saving his life.

"Will you allow me to film you?" I asked Lale one day. "Nothing lengthy, just a short chat with me."

He agreed with a nonchalant, "Whatever, if it helps you tell my story."

I asked my two sons to put together a small film crew and hire a studio. The morning of filming didn't start well. I had also asked my eighteen-year-old daughter to be part of the film, walk on, attach a lapel microphone to Lale, to set up the interview. She was to incur the wrath of her mother by turning up late and hungover. Lale, however, always her biggest fan, made a fuss of her, praising her for living her life to the fullest and telling her it was good she was upsetting her mother, that was her job.

Five young people—producer, director, sound, camera, and the wayward daughter—focus when the director says "Action!" The scene unfolds. I stop, waiting for the word "Cut!" Nothing. I look behind me at the crew—all are stunned, speechless at what they have just seen and heard. The camera rolls. "Cut!" I finally say. I see the tears in my daughter's eyes as she looks in admiration at this amazing old man. Slowly, as one, they move toward Lale. Bending down, they hug him, pat him on the back, shake his hand—they have fallen under his spell. "You're living history," I hear one of them murmur. They got it—they got Lale. For two hours, we stayed in that studio. Five young adults wanting to hear more, listening with open hearts and minds. Lale was in his happy place, being the center of attention with a willing audience listening intently. I remember feeling a tad jealous when I observed his reaction when one of them interrupted to ask a question: "Good, good!" he said. "You heard me, you want to know more, I'll tell you."

There were several elements of Lale's time in Auschwitz-Birkenau he struggled to talk about. Some of them I knew nothing about for nearly a year into our friendship. Others he touched on, pursed his lips, shook his head, and shut down. I knew to say nothing. Not to prod him into remembering, just to leave him be. If he wanted me to know certain things, he would tell me in his own good time. I've often wondered how many untold memories he took to his grave. It doesn't matter—that was his decision, his right.

If you have read *The Tattooist of Auschwitz*, you will know that Lale spent time living in the part of Auschwitz-Birkenau designated the Gypsy camp. Of course, the correct term should be Roma camp. That is not the name it was referred to as at the time, nor by Lale, and I make no judgment on him calling it the "Gypsy camp." This period of his time in Auschwitz-Birkenau was one of those story lines he held on to tightly.

And then one day he didn't. As always with Lale, he told me bits of stories, names of prisoners or SS officers; dates and times of a historically important horror he witnessed and, in some cases, experienced. I have written about his relationship with the Gypsy families, but what you do not know is the level of pain Lale felt then and relived, telling me as I sat quietly, listening to his quavering voice, watching him wipe tears from his eyes with hands that shook. The physical pain I felt sitting, listening to him, still affects me greatly. Lale had the courage to finally talk about it; I would simply write my notes within a few hours of hearing him. In writing up my notes, I would see his face—turned away from me, Tootsie and Bam Bam curled up at his feet—staring at a space on the far wall until he was finished. Then he got up and walked to the painting hanging behind him, standing only a few feet away from the gift Gita had given him when they were living in Bratislava after the war: the painting of the Gypsy woman. This is what he told me:

I'm stalling finishing off my story about the Gypsies. I don't want to finish this story, it's too painful. History has recorded what happened to them in a one-line sentence—I will take only a few more.

I was there. I heard the screams as they were woken in the middle of the night and ordered out of their blocks. I got up and watched as my friends called out to me to save them. I couldn't know at the time exactly what was going to happen to them, but I had a good idea. Four and a half thousand men, women, and children were pushed, beaten, and shoved into the backs of large trucks. I ran outside and confronted an SS standing by one of the trucks, pleading with him to leave them alone, not to take the women and children. He raised his rifle at me and told me if I didn't go back inside, he would put me on the truck with them.

I watched them walk past me as I stood in the doorway. They walked past me with their heads held high, proud. Many of the men shook my hand, the women simply said goodbye. When Natya got to me, I begged her to simply stay behind, telling her that I would find a way to protect her. She smiled at me and said she had to go with her people.

Within a very short period of time I stood alone, now the only occupant of the Gypsy camp. I had never felt so helpless. The night dragged on, the new day dawned, gray and foreboding and bringing me more work. I had become very good at knowing approximately what time of the day it was, so when I say it was late morning, I'm talking 11–11:30 a.m., when working frantically with the newest arrivals I felt the familiar sting of ash falling on my face. Within a few minutes the sky turned dark and the ash of four and a half thousand Gypsies rained down on me. I know I dropped to my knees; I know I shed tears. One of my assistants, alarmed that I was sick, assisted me to my feet.

"Lale, Lale, what's wrong?" he said.

As he helped me up, I looked over to where the selections were being made and saw Mengele looking at me. He walked over.

"Are you sick, Tätowierer?"

I shook my head, picked up my tattoo stick, and reached for the next victim's arm.

Mengele smiled at me.

"One day, Tätowierer, one day I will take you."

History and memory. I've written about it previously. I remain convinced that when listening to someone relate experiences they witnessed personally and were part of, it is the individual's memory and recollection that takes precedence over the accounts told by others who did not personally bear witness. Nonetheless, I decided that in telling Lale and Gita's story, I would only include events that could be corroborated by another piece of evidence, particularly when it related to people other than Lale. That was the rule

I set for myself. I was writing fiction, but given the subject matter, I felt that it had to be grounded in fact and if I could not verify it by a secondary account, I left it out. One particular instance of this stays with me. Lale talked about an incident involving Czesław Mordowicz, a significant prisoner, a man whose story has been widely told without any reference to Lale. A professional researcher had spoken to the Mordowicz family and they insisted they had not heard of Lale Sokolov, that their father had never mentioned he knew him, and that Lale had played no part in Mordowicz's time in Auschwitz-Birkenau.

When Lale first read a copy of my original screenplay, he got cranky with me: "Where is my Mordowicz story? Why haven't you written about him?" I know he was unhappy with my explanation of not being able to verify his account. He relayed the story to me many times and I sat and listened, believing him wholeheartedly. I knew him so well and felt certain that his version of what he called his "Mordowicz story" was 100 percent true to his memory.

When *The Tattooist of Auschwitz* was eventually published in 2018, it did not contain the Mordowicz story because I was unable to verify it with anyone other than Lale. My novel was released in many countries and I started to receive emails from around the world. One of those emails came from a journalist in Canada, who wrote telling me that he had read my book while writing a belated obituary for Czesław Mordowicz. He had a copy of Mordowicz's translated testimony regarding his escape from Auschwitz-Birkenau and told me Mordowicz had written about the part Lale Sokolov had played in his escape. He sent me a photo of the elderly Mordowicz, holding his left arm out for the camera. You will understand the significance of this as you read on.

As I read the testimony, I heard Lale telling me the same story. He was gone; his story was written, but I wanted to tell him: *I never doubted you, Lale. I hope you understood in the end why I couldn't put this incident in your book. I had listened to you telling me so many times. I know you would have loved it to be part of your novel. I can tell it now.*

* * *

To understand Lale's small role in the life of Czesław Mordowicz, I need to tell you a little of this man and his significance in the story of the Holocaust.

Czesław Mordowicz, prisoner 84216, escaped from

Auschwitz-Birkenau with another prisoner, Arnost Rosin, on May 27, 1944. They made their way to Slovakia, where they met up with two other young men, Rudolf Vrba and Alfred Wetzler, who had escaped in April 1944. Vrba and Wetzler had compiled a report for the Slovakian Jewish Council regarding the role Auschwitz-Birkenau played as an extermination camp. Mordowicz and Rosin not only corroborated the information and details given but added the horrific details that 100,000 Jewish men, women, and children had arrived in Birkenau from Hungary, most of whom were taken immediately to the gas chamber. These reports have subsequently been titled "The Auschwitz Protocols." The document was smuggled to Switzerland and the Vatican. It made its way to the United States. Both the *New York Times* and the BBC in London reported on its contents. The document is credited with generating sufficient public pressure that the Hungarian government halted the deportation of its Jewish citizens in July 1944. By this time, approximately 430,000 Hungarian-Jewish men, women, and children had been deported.

In August 1944, the Slovakian uprising took place, as resistance fighters attempted unsuccessfully to overthrow the German troops occupying Slovakia.

Mordowicz was captured and returned to Auschwitz-Birkenau. On his way back to Poland, he attempted to chew his tattooed number off his arm. He knew the penalty for escape was to be publicly executed as a deterrent; all prisoners in Auschwitz-Birkenau were tattooed on the left arm and when his time came to be either tattooed or inspected by a doctor or SS man during selection, his number would be noted.

Lale heard about Mordowicz and went to see him with two other prisoners from Slovakia as soon as he arrived at the camp. Mordowicz tells a simple story of Lale changing his tattooed number into a flower. Lale tells of a young man with an infected, very unpleasant wound with the numbers still visible enough to be identified. He told me of the bravery Mordowicz showed as Lale tattooed over the shredded and infected skin to create a rose. It was a flower to Mordowicz; for Lale, it was the symbol of love—a rose, not just any flower.

As a result of Lale's action, Mordowicz was able to remain undetected in Birkenau and survive the Holocaust. He and Lale caught up again back in Bratislava, Slovakia, after the war. While Lale moved to Australia to live, Mordowicz moved to Canada.

I tell this story because Lale was so proud to have

known and helped in a small way one of the four brave men who escaped from Auschwitz-Birkenau and had the courage to write what they had witnessed and experienced, convincing the Slovakian Jewish Council of its accuracy, who in turn took the risk to smuggle the document out of the country to neutral Switzerland. While I had listened to Lale tell me this story many, many times, it wasn't until I received the proof from Canada that I felt able to write this story of his.

When I think about Lale and my great-grandfather, I cannot find one similarity between the two men. Gramps was over six feet tall—a big built man, even in his eighties. Lale was eighty-seven when I met him, no more than five and a half feet tall and a strong wind could blow him over. On a couple of occasions when I visited him, I found him black-and-blue from bruises after his doggies had pulled away from him on a walk and he'd fallen. His skin was translucent, his bruises—which he brushed off and wouldn't let me tend to—all the more stark. Lale loved to laugh, had a sparkle in his eye, and was a complete and utter flirt with any female he met. Gramps was reserved, thoughtful, each word chosen carefully—I cannot remember him ever laughing. Lale telling his story was rambling, waffling, no connection between sentences. I could spend several hours with him and learn nothing new, he just loved to talk. We made a good team, I loved to listen. The only thing that connected the two men was me and my love of spending time with older people, appreciating their life experiences, humbled that they would share them with me.

3

How to Listen

The word "listen" contains the same letters as the word "silent."

The biggest communication problem is that we do not listen to understand; we listen to reply.

Should be simple, right? When you are in the company of at least one other person and they are talking, then surely you must be listening? However, all too often we are not listening to learn something new. Instead, our brains are frantically picking and choosing only part of what is being said to us, the part we want to respond to, comment on, share an opinion on. Often, we are very focused on what we want to say and looking for the opening in which to say it. Watch yourself next time you are in a conversation—we all do it and it's not a criticism to point this out. Often listening is merely a pause in a transaction in which we take turns to download what each of us wants to say and often it's linked to a particular impression we are trying to make, or very much grounded in the nature of the conversation. This is sometimes called "phatic communication"—verbal interaction, the basis of which is a social function rather than the actual transfer of information. And mostly, if a casual conversation is all that is warranted—a chat over the fence with a neighbor, for example—then this partial listening is perfectly fine. An exchange about the weather, health, how one's weekend went, how the family are—all can be done pretty much on autopilot. If, however, we should be listening because the person speaking to us wishes to share something personal and meaningful to them, that requires a whole different form of listening—*real* listening. And I believe that this skill, this art of listening, has diminished in the busy, socially disconnected world in which we now live.

Listening starts when we are born. Some say before we are born, and studies now tell us unborn fetuses hear sound. How many parents-to-be have spent many intimate moments talking to their unborn babies, through their partner's bellies, believing they will recognize their voice when they meet? I've done it myself to my daughter, wanting to connect to my unborn grandchildren, two of whom I was present to witness take their first breath and whisper words of love moments after their births.

Being a grandmother has given me an opportunity to observe, listen, and learn from little people; an opportunity that, in the exhaustion, sleep deprivation, and anxiety of being a new parent myself, passed me by. Nothing gives me more joy than listening to these little people telling me stories of their days, explaining to me what they are doing. However, it is easy to lose focus, not concentrate, with repercussions.

My grandsons are currently obsessed with LEGO. My daughter calls her son's LEGO catalog his "bible." Throughout the day, he can be found studying this ratty-looking booklet, the pages no longer contained by staples. I watch his brain building the LEGO constructions he dreams of owning. At night, when we peek into his bedroom, hoping he is asleep, he can be found sitting in the dark with a small flashlight, turning the pages, running his fingers over the pictures. He knows how many bags of LEGO each construction will have and shares this statistic with anyone willing to listen. I thought I was doing a good job listening to his dreams of ownership and how long it would take him to create the Harry Potter castle and many others, being an active listener and participant. Clearly, there had been a moment when I wasn't paying full attention, and this I learned when he told me he couldn't wait for the shops to reopen so we could get the (very expensive) double roller coaster I'd seemingly promised I would buy him.

What I have observed is how even the very young can choose not to listen. Recently, I heard my five-year-old grandson talking to his three-year-old sister, saying, "Rachy, you're not listening to me, *listen to me*, Rachy!" I went over to the two of them. They had been playing together, now Rachy had turned her back on him. I asked my grandson what the problem was, and he answered, "Rachy isn't listening to me." Then I asked Rachel if she had heard her brother. She nodded. Big brother interrupted with, "You're not listening to me." Stubborn Little Miss Three-Year-Old responded forcefully, "I don't want to listen to you." I explained to big brother that his sister was perfectly entitled not to listen to him, and he couldn't make her. He accepted this with a maturity beyond his years and asked her if she would listen to him later. She said she would, and he was satisfied.

What I loved about this exchange was the lack of ambiguity and pretense. Little Miss Three-Year-Old wanted to do something else. Her brother learned that it was pointless trying to push his demands; he would come back to it later. As adults, I believe we don't make our feelings as obvious when we may not be in the mood to listen. We say nothing, shut down, but the person talking to us doesn't always know this. It's called communication, or in many instances, *failure* to communicate. Failure to be sensitive to the needs of someone when they want to talk to us. Failure on the part of the speaker in recognizing the needs of the other person to acknowledge that we each need to be in the right place and time to hear something they may be desperate to share.

I am as guilty as the next person of not reading the body language or verbal comments that indicate someone is wanting to tell me something that they need me to hear. It does not matter how close or intimate you may be with someone, even your nearest and dearest will not know 100 percent of the time what headspace you are in, or even what has happened to you in the preceding minutes, hours, or days. For we may not have communicated it to them in such a way that they were able to hear.

It all comes down to the first few words we say when we want someone to listen, not to advise, just listen. I've learned that the words "Can I tell you something?" are the best way to get attention. Maybe the other person thinks I am going to tell them a secret, but it works for me. Of course, time and place are a major factor when needing someone to truly listen to you, but equally, it's essential to ask to be heard. What follows are the basic elements of listening, as I understand them—again, I write not as an expert but rather from experience—as a parent, a partner, a sibling, a social worker, and more recently, as a writer.

Active Listening

This sounds odd, doesn't it? How do you *not* listen actively? Well, the short answer is that it's not as easy nor as obvious as it sounds. This is not, in my opinion, the listening we do all the time, every time we are in conversation with someone. But the basic ideas and techniques of active listening can be learned and practiced, and they will make us all better listeners.

The key idea behind active listening is to focus concentration entirely on the speaker, to give them the space and encouragement to tell you what they want you to hear. This is a different transaction from the phatic communication I was talking about earlier in this chapter, where you and the neighbor exchange hellos and chat about your weekends—there, the aim is simply positive communication.

The basic rules of active listening are: to concentrate, to understand, to respond, to remember what is being said, to withhold judgment or opinion.

Whenever I sat with Lale, I switched on my active listening skills. It took time for me to earn his trust and I knew I'd done so the day that Tootsie gave me the ball to throw. We'd relaxed into a place where he knew I was there, ready to hear what he most urgently needed to relate, that I was open to hearing it. I believe that he'd decided that I would be the one; he knew that I was prepared to hear his story, that I understood the importance of it—and that I would not judge. When we were in proper speaking and listening mode, after an initial exchange of pleasantries, with those yummy wafers and that terrible coffee, I focused only on his words. I made a conscious effort not to hear only the words he was saying but to hear the complete message he was communicating with each sentence, each story.

I never took any recording device, not even pen and paper, to my meetings with Lale. I call them "meetings," not "interviews." Interviews are a two-way street—question, answer. I had determined on the first day I met Lale that any movement or interruption on my part distracted him and he lost the thread of what he was saying. You have to remember: he was eighty-seven years old and grieving terribly. I listened intently, committed to memory names and places to be written down as soon as I got home. This had its funny sides at times when Lale slipped into a language I did not understand. Slovakian, Russian, German . . . they all got a go. I said nothing and Lale would realize what he was doing, have a little giggle and I never knew if he then repeated in English what I had just missed.

I would write down in bullet points what I had taken from each of our meetings. Phonetically spell names and places, write them in a small notebook for later clarification. It was easy at the end of our time together to simply produce the notebook and casually ask, "Last time I saw you, you mentioned someone called . . ." He would laugh at my attempt at pronouncing foreign names. I would then joke with him, call him a smarty-pants, and push the notebook in front of him and ask him to "spell it for me, then." These conversations only happened after I had realized it was time to move him away from telling his story, that he was tired, growing distressed or anxious. Until then, it was all about him talking and me listening.

This, quite simply, was paying full attention to him, not allowing any distraction to break the spell I let him put me under. I was never at risk of being bored, but there were many instances when my concentration left me. Many of the things Lale told me about his time in Auschwitz-Birkenau were of him witnessing pure evil, violent, brutal, and horrific acts perpetrated by the Nazis. As I scrambled to comprehend what I was hearing, often failing, I would see his lips moving and realize that he was talking, but I was no longer hearing. It was as if I was drowning in the horror. I had learned early in our relationship not to interrupt Lale and ask him to repeat something, or explain a detail, who someone was. If I did, he would lose his way in the story he was telling and become agitated. This made it difficult for me to listen to him at the level I needed to be able to race home and write up what he had just been telling me. I would become fixed in a visual place of horror that was difficult to move away from. After a few times of this happening, I instinctively put a hand down beside me, knowing there would be a doggy asleep between Lale and me. Patting and scratching the head of whichever dog lay at my feet returned me to the present time and place. Lale was none the wiser that I had ever "left" him—I was back listening.

Animals—pets, in particular—provide us with unconditional comfort. All the times I stayed up until the early hours of the morning writing, the full-time day job preventing me from following my love of writing during "normal" working hours, it was my dog Lucy who sat, slept mostly, at my feet. As with Lale and his doggies, I would reach down and pat her, turn to her if she raised her head, woken by my touch, and share a moment before I resumed my writing and she went back to sleep. *Until next time.* As a child, I never had a pet. Dogs were working dogs, cats to keep the mice from the house and food sheds.

It sounds weird, but I got my animal comfort from cows. Is there a gentler animal? Walking through a paddock of grazing cows, looking them in the eyes, we were the same height—patting and talking to them was my comfort zone.

During my years working in the social work department of a large hospital—between 1995 and 2017—I was confronted by unbearable pain and suffering. We are currently celebrating doctors and nurses as heroes as they work long, demanding hours trying to save the lives of far too many people struck down with COVID-19. It seems like the rest of the world has woken up to what I always knew: it is not our politicians and sports people who should be crowned legends and heroes; it is medical staff. There is one other group of professionals working in hospitals that I place on the highest pedestal—social workers. I was not one; I worked with them. Supported and assisted them in the difficult times. As we used to joke, no one comes to see a social worker because they are having a good day! They now find themselves supporting family and friends who cannot be with loved ones in their final hours. Can you imagine what that must be like? To have to hold, comfort, and be with mothers, fathers, husbands, wives, children, siblings, friends as they learn their loved ones have died. But there is another aspect to what these incredible people do. After the family and friends have left the hospital, often it is the very nurses and doctors who tried to save lives who come to their ward social worker for debriefing and comfort.

For over twenty years, I was privileged to be called an honorary social worker and to be trusted to provide care, comfort, and support to thousands of patients and their families—mostly, their families. I had a role providing accommodation and support to family and friends of patients who lived a long distance from the hospital: I cared for the carers. In front of me as I write, hanging on my wall, is a painting done by a young woman, barely twenty-one years of age. I had known her and her family—mostly her mother— for five or six years, seeing them all too often. The patient passed her time, when she was able, painting. Three days before she died, she had her mother wheel her to my office so she could give me a painting she had made specially for me. Quite possibly, the last work she ever painted. Looking at it is incredibly painful for me. To *not* look at it each day would be more painful. When she handed it to me and told me what it meant to her, I said nothing. I thanked her with a hug. I could see she was distressed and nodded to her mother to take her back to her bed—it was time to let her go and be with the people that mattered most in her life. I will be always grateful to her family for allowing her to come and see me and I treasure the artwork she made for me.

There was always that one moment when I would deliberately interrupt Lale and that was when I decided he was getting upset and needed to leave 1944 behind and come back to the present. I would notice signs of agitation. The foot tapping and avoiding my eye were there, but Lale also had a way of pursing his lips and shaking his head from side to side, opening and closing his eyes, that told me enough was enough—for now, time to shut him down. During my years working with patients and families I learned to recognize many signs and mannerisms that indicated we had reached a time when distress and trauma had reached a peak and a person's need to keep talking was at an end. This varied incredibly and no time frame could be put on it. For some people, ten minutes was all they could manage, talking of extremely traumatic or tragic circumstances. For others, well, let's just say, many lunch breaks didn't happen as I stayed in the moment with someone whose need to speak overwhelmed them. To have someone listening without being personally connected to them unleashed a torrent of past and present concerns.

There were instances with Lale when I got my timing wrong. He would tell me in no uncertain terms that he needed to finish telling me something, it was important to get it out. When I told him that I was worried about him and perhaps it was time to stop, that I could see that he had become physically and emotionally distraught, he would quietly tell me he needed to become emotional, how else could he tell me of the horror he had witnessed and experienced? How could he expect me to write about him if he didn't go back there and experience it again? Of course, he was right. It then became a juggling act for me. I had to let my instincts dictate whether to let him continue when every bone in my body told me to stop him, not to let him suffer any more that day.

I had two avenues for bringing Lale back to his immaculate living room, back to his place of safety, to the here and now. Suggesting to him that his doggies might like us to take them for a walk always worked. Lale lived in what could be considered a predominantly Jewish suburb. There were families walking around the streets at all times of the day and night.

From the younger families we always got smiles, nods of the head, and a greeting depending on the time of the day. Many times we ran into friends of Lale and we would chat for as long as the doggies would stay still, until a tug on their leads, particularly Tootsie's, propelled us forward.

I always loved it when someone would call out to him from the other side of the road, "*Tätowierer*, how are you?" Many knew Lale as the *Tätowierer* in Auschwitz-Birkenau and greeted him accordingly. Given his age, our walks were not long—no more than thirty minutes. Lale knew exactly when to turn around and head back home.

If the weather was inclement, or Lale wasn't feeling up to a walk, usually in the evening when he was tired, then bringing up any of the current sports being played locally or internationally also did the trick. He loved sports. If his television was on when I arrived, it was always sports he had been watching. There were times when Lale and Gita's son Gary would join us and he would share with me stories of growing up and what his father had told him about the Holocaust. What I particularly loved hearing from him were stories about his mother. A parent–child relationship is quite different to a couple's relationship. It was obvious he had grown up in a loving supportive family. While his mother told him very little about her time during the Holocaust, her love and affection for her son radiated from him.

Was Lale an active listener? He could be, but mostly he liked to do the talking and we both knew I was there to listen. One subject he listened intently to me about was the trials and tribulations I was experiencing with my young adult daughter. He wanted to know what she had been doing since we last met, was she still with the same boyfriend (whom he had met), as he didn't consider him good enough for her. When I shared with him some of her antics and my concerns for her, he would laugh loudly, asking to see her so he could encourage her to rattle her mother further. He was also very good at wanting to give me parenting advice, always prefacing it with "I never had a daughter, I don't really know how to bring one up, but if I did, this is what I would do . . ." Then he would proceed to give me his considered opinion. He was particularly concerned that she should not drink alcohol—he had seen too many young girls affected by it, placing themselves in danger by not being fully aware. He wanted my assurance I would advise her of his opinion. She had chosen not to enter tertiary education, which he considered a mistake, and suggested I work harder to convince her to reconsider. I loved how he could embrace my family, ask meaningful questions, and be sensitive to my concerns when dealing with a problem involving them. I always felt completely safe sharing with him details of my life, knowing he respected my privacy. While I didn't always take his advice, I knew it came from the heart and was always well intentioned. And I relished having someone to talk to who wasn't in any way connected to them.

Each time I arrived for one of our meetings, he greeted me with the words, "Have you finished my book yet?" And each time I gave him the same answer: "No, Lale, and I'm not writing a book, I'm writing a screenplay." There was no follow-up from him to my response for nearly a year and then one day, he turned to me with a puzzled look on his face and said, "What's a screenplay?"

We had made it from the front door into his lounge room and I knew his next move would be to head to the kitchen to make me another cup of bad coffee. Tootsie and Bam Bam had already headed there—they knew the ritual. But Lale paused to hear my answer, so they had to double back.

"Well, Lale, I'm writing your story in the hope it will be made into a film—I want to see your story told as a movie."

The look on his face was priceless.

"A movie, you want to make a movie about me and Gita?" he blurted out.

"Yes, I do, your love story rivals *Romeo and Juliet*," I told him. "The power of your story compares with the greatest films ever made about courage and survival, so yes, I would love your story to be a movie."

His next words were not what I was expecting, though in retrospect as I think back on this charming, delightful, self-assured elderly man, they were perfect.

"Well, who will play me?" he asked.

"I don't know, Lale. We're not there yet, I'm just writing your story as a screenplay in the hope that one day, someone will want to make it into a movie."

The surprises kept coming.

"Brad Pitt, you get me Brad Pitt! He's a good-looking boy, *I'm* a good-looking boy!"

Unable to contain my laughter, I hugged him, telling him he was indeed a very good-looking boy, as was Brad Pitt, but he was too old to play him. *Sorry, Brad!*

Accepting what I was saying, Lale then told me we had to find the perfect person to play Lale Sokolov because he wanted to know who it would be before he joined Gita, so he could tell her when they were together again.

I offered to bring my laptop around one day so he and I could look at all the young actors currently available for his consideration. *No, that was not what we were going to do. We would go to the cinema.* He wanted to see the actors before he made his decision.

Ultimately, my daughter was to play a pivotal role in Lale finding the actor he wanted to "play him." She worked at a large cinema multiplex and knew every new movie that was coming out and could get us tickets to sit back and analyze the male actors.

Movie after movie we went to. On several occasions I had to get permission from my boss to have an afternoon away from the hospital to accommodate Lale—he wasn't keen on going out at night. We'd be greeted by my daughter and given a coffee (made by a barista, so I certainly welcomed it), and she would sit with us for a while before escorting Lale to his seat.

"What about him?" I would say as a young, good-looking boy appeared on the screen in front of us. While I would whisper, Lale always responded in a loud voice: "What are you thinking?" were his chosen words. On hearing this, I knew to sit back, relax, and enjoy the movie. Only on our drive back to his place would he give me his reasons for rejecting the actor. Often, he said they weren't tall enough. I kept my smile to myself—Lale's image of himself as six feet tall was not borne out by the old man I was spending time with, nor any photos of the young Lale I had seen.

Another day, another movie. Driving there, I was telling Lale about the actor James Marsden, who I thought would be perfect to play him: tall, dark, and handsome. He was, as usual, noncommittal, but brightened up when he met my daughter and got to spend time with her. I always felt like a third wheel when they were together, but also enjoyed immensely the spark in his eyes and how much she loved being with what we as a family called living history.

As the lights went down and the film began, I was certain today was going to be the day. The movie had just been released and the cinema was full. Within a few minutes, James Marsden was on the screen: tall, dark, and handsome, as promised. I dug Lale in the ribs, whispering, "That's him, he's you!" It was dark, but I could tell he rolled his eyes, then said those familiar words, "What are you thinking?"

Fail. I had failed again. Sit back and relax. Then it happened. Cut to a new scene, a new leading male. Lale jumped to his feet.

"That's me, that's me, he should be me!" he screamed out.

Pulling him down into his seat, I shushed him. He remained shushed for only a few minutes before once again standing up.

"You, down the front, turn around and look at me! Don't you think he looks like me?" he shouted out.

As I was pulling him back down, he was still calling out. Being shushed by others was working. Then someone started slow clapping and many others joined in. Lale now whispered to me, "See, they agree with me, he should be me!" *Yes, Lale.* We had now found the perfect person to play Lale Sokolov: Ryan Gosling. With Lale now shushed, everyone in the cinema got to enjoy the wonderful movie, *The Notebook.*

Sometime previously, Lale had seen a film starring the actress Natalie Portman. To him, she was the only person who could possibly play Gita.

He had good taste, our Lale.

That is how he often referred to himself, by his full name—Lale Sokolov—although I soon learned that Sokolov was not his surname until 1945. Having survived the Holocaust, Lale returned to Communist-controlled Czechoslovakia and created a successful business importing fabrics: linen, silk, wool, and lace. He was a supplier to clothing manufacturing businesses, the majority of which were owned either by the state or private, non-Jewish individuals. His birth surname of Eisenberg began to create problems for him as antisemitism continued to be rife in his home country. He felt he was losing out on contracts because he was being identified first and foremost as a Jew rather than the successful businessman he saw himself as. His sister Goldie, his only surviving family member, married a Russian soldier at the end of the war and took his surname of Sokolov. Lale made the decision to change his name to that also. In his hometown of Krompachy, the mayor showed me the large journal with his birth registration written. At the end of the document there is a notation that Lale had visited the town hall and requested that he be known as Sokolov.

That even one member of his family had survived was something of a miracle. Lale was the baby in his family, a self-confessed mama's boy. He looked up to his older brother, Max, who didn't survive the Holocaust, but he was closest to his sister Goldie. In many ways, he said, she was a second mother to him. She cared for him when he was small and his mother was busy, walking him to school until he decided that he was old enough to walk on his own. The day Lale boarded the train bound for Auschwitz in April 1942, Goldie remained in the family home in Krompachy. She was still there when he returned in May 1945. Goldie had been cared for, hidden, moved from household to household, and never turned over to the Nazis by the locals.

Lale was in my life for almost three years. Did we always talk about his time as the *Tätowierer* in Auschwitz-Birkenau? No, far from it. We were soon friends and our conversations could be about anything. I started learning about his and Gita's life after liberation, back in Slovakia under Communist rule, their escape, and subsequent life in Australia.

Escape. A word you associate with imprisonment.

That is exactly where Lale was, *in prison*. He had become very successful as an importer of fine fabrics. Russian businessmen moved into Czechoslovakia, bringing their families—in particular, their wives. Lale tapped into a previously nonexistent market providing fabrics for clothing manufacturers. With success came a need to give back. Lale chose to share his wealth not in his home country but through secretly transferring funds to Jewish contacts in Palestine to fight for a free Israel. He was caught, charged, tried, and sentenced to a spell in Ilava Prison. His and Gita's apartment was taken from them, their bank accounts emptied—all possessions now belonged to the government. Gita moved in with friends. However, Lale being Lale, he had hidden funds which only Gita knew about.

Bribing a judge, Gita was introduced to a psychiatrist and together, they hatched a plan to get Lale leave from his prison sentence. A Catholic priest was next to receive an envelope from Gita. Visiting Lale in prison, the priest told him he had to start going "mad." When the prison authorities asked for a psychiatrist to assess him via the court, the "bribed" psychiatrist visited and told the authorities Lale needed weekend leave to prevent him from becoming permanently "mad." I am telling you this using the words Lale used when telling me this story.

With weekend leave granted, friends helped Lale and Gita escape to Vienna hidden in the false wall of a produce truck. Taking one suitcase each, Gita insisted on taking the painting of a Gypsy woman she had bought as a gift for Lale. From Vienna, they made their way to Paris, where they stayed for several months. Unable to find work, they decided to leave Europe and go to the furthermost country they knew: Australia. Lale obtained false passports and they duly arrived in Australia in 1949. Lale never left Australia again. Gita, however, traveled back to Slovakia several times to see her two brothers, who had became partisans and fought with the Russians and survived the war, and also her friend Cilka Klein, with whom she stayed in contact her entire life. She also visited Israel.

In Australia, Lale and Gita began once more from scratch, again working in textiles. Sometimes the going was good, sometimes things didn't pan out and he'd begin again, he told me. He always worked, always made ends meet—didn't worry too much about what the work was, so long as he was providing for his family.

When Lale told me these stories, such as his escape with Gita, he was excited and proud of how she had taken initiative in securing his release. He would often change tack and tell me something extraordinary and new and this was a challenge for me—I'd have to really concentrate to stay on track. I had no control over what he would talk about on any given day; I could not direct him to fill in gaps of previous stories or explain something in more detail. No, Lale was going to tell me what he wanted to talk about. He alone decided the topic of conversation. It was my role to actively listen to whatever he was throwing at me, look for a reason in the spaces between the words for why he felt the need to change topic—what was it that he had been talking about that sent him down the path of a different recollection? Sometimes it was obvious, and I saw the link; often I didn't, so I simply accepted his need to go to another place and time.

It was important that I remain alert to all the ingredients of being an active listener. The obvious ones I had practiced our entire friendship. I was always watching his body language, the tapping of his feet as his agitation grew; turning his face from me when the memories, the remembering, was painful; the twinkle in his eye as he fully made eye contact with me and spoke of his love for Gita. Oh, how I loved listening to him tell me about their annual holidays on the Gold Coast in Queensland, Australia.

They would go to the beach every day and he would be overwhelmed by the beauty of seeing Gita in a bathing suit, enjoying the sun and sand. These holidays were the highlight of his year, when the two of them would truly relax and be there for each other. "No distractions," he would say. No one bothered him, asked anything of him; they spent twenty-four hours a day together, living the life denied to both their families. He told me that this was the one simple thing that connected them to their lost loved ones: living their best life. The single tear that would escape was a tear of joy. It was not difficult to be fully attentive and in the moment with him—it was an honor and privilege to be the person with whom he shared these memories. The good and the bad. The painful, the beautiful. I would like to think I conveyed to him how I felt being with him, how special it was to me. I can only presume he knew—he never stopped wanting to see me, talk to me, tell me his stories of hope.

There was no doubt Lale lived with what I consider to be a degree of "survivor guilt." It is my (unprofessional) opinion that every Holocaust survivor I have met and spoken with carries survivor guilt to some extent. It was obvious in Lale when he spoke about his family—he told me how he and Gita often acknowledged the unfairness of surviving when most of their family members had not. He would remind her of the vow they made to each other: the only way they could honor all those who did not survive the Holocaust was to live the best life they could.

Lale, fearing the Czechoslovakian authorities would arrest him if he left Australia, chose never to leave. As he and Gita worked, they saved money to send to Goldie, who remained in Czechoslovakia, and when it became possible for her to travel, he paid for her to fly to Australia to spend precious time with them.

He loved to tell me about the first time he flew Goldie to Australia. Melbourne did not have an international airport and she had to fly into Sydney. He did what he thought was the right thing and flew to Sydney to meet her and bring her to their home. For several hours he paced around Sydney airport without finding her. Eventually he rang Gita to say she must have missed the flight, terrified something might have happened to her. Gita apparently let him talk about what he should do, how he could find out what had become of her, before putting Goldie on the phone. It seems his sister wasn't as useless as Lale thought she was. Arriving in Sydney, she knew she had to fly to Melbourne, so she bought a ticket, flew down, got in a taxi, and knocked on the door, thankful that Gita was home. Lale was forced to stay the night in Sydney and the reunion was delayed by twenty-four hours.

I have told you how, as I sat in Lale's living room, at a café, driving in my car with him, walking his doggies, whenever I was listening to him, I never recorded him or made notes. Under normal circumstances if, say, a journalist or historian was getting a story, they would record the conversation and also make notes. Instinctively, I felt any distraction, be it the whirring of a machine or my note taking and doodling (*I do doodle!*) would be an interruption with consequences. But I was hearing names and places, details of a time in history I had admitted ashamedly to Lale I knew little about. For me there was a tension between my role as listener and the job of getting down the story, which was equally important—to him, and increasingly to me. What Lale needed was someone to listen to him, just to be there as he spoke of a time and a place he had kept locked away for decades, that reliving it at the end of his life had become essential and therapeutic. But he also felt the hand of history on his shoulder—that beneath all the jokes about Ryan Gosling and Natalie Portman, this old man knew he had played a role that needed to be recorded for the future. He knew that sharing these stories was essential to ensuring that it never happened again. And I in turn felt an enormous responsibility both as his confidante and the person he had chosen to entrust with his story.

After I left Lale, I always went directly home. Often dinner would be delayed as I went to my computer and tried to make a comprehensive record of our time together. I wrote names and places down phonetically and I'd then try to match them with real names and places—my library of Holocaust literature was growing day by day. Using the dates Lale had given me of the events he had witnessed and been part of, I would search the internet and books for further information. Slowly, little by little, I began to flesh out his narrative. This was my role as chronicler of Lale's story. In my other role, as the person chosen to listen to him, I created the spreadsheet I described earlier, in which I kept note of his mental state on each visit.

I had been told by a friend who is a mental health professional, that Lale would never tell me anything he didn't want me to know. I had asked his opinion because I feared doing harm in having Lale remember and talk about such a traumatic past. My friend reminded me always to "shut him down" before leaving him, making sure he was happily in the present, and this I took care to do in the ways I've described. The spreadsheet enabled me to keep track of how I found him and how I left him. I also included a brief note on how I was affected by my visits and what I was hearing and absorbing in my time with him.

One of the most important aspects of being a social worker or in other therapeutic roles is regular "supervision" sessions with an experienced colleague. In these meetings, work practice can be discussed, concerns voiced, and support and encouragement given. While my relationship with Lale was in no way a therapeutic one, I am so grateful to my boss—who possibly now knows as much about Lale as I do—for allowing me to open up to her. I'll describe a bit more about the cost of listening later in this book.

Before I set out to see Lale each time, I would write

down the names and places I had found in my research that seemed to connect to what Lale had told me and a list of things I felt I needed to know. I would keep this in my handbag until I was getting ready to leave, when we'd wound down with a dog walk or a chat, and it was time to say goodbye. Only then would I take the piece of paper out and ask a specific question—one or two at most. "Was the commandant you talked about last time Schwarzhuber or Kramer?" for instance, or "When did you think it was you first met Mengele?" or "What was the name of the town Gita came from?" When I asked him something in this manner, after he had been talking uninterrupted for hours and we had broken the spell by walking the doggies or discussing who would win Wimbledon, he'd reply casually, eyes cast into the distance. I think he knew exactly why I was asking these questions, but he never commented on it. Also, he always had the answer at his fingertips—his memory was razor-sharp and unfailingly accurate. And so, piece by piece, day by day, month by month, I was given, and received, the story of *The Tattooist of Auschwitz.*

I had a story, a story I now needed to write. A story I believed others would want to hear, or as I was writing it as a screenplay, see. My life and Lale's had become entwined: neither one of us could advance without the other. Lale had such faith in my ability to tell his story and his encouragement was a tonic that enabled me to do my very best writing, that gave me the confidence to seek to tell his story. My family supported me unconditionally, friends and work colleagues hung on to every word when I shared stories from Lale. While I didn't realize it at the time, Lale telling me his story, and my listening to it, became a story in itself. However, I always emphasize that while the novel may be mine and bear my name, *The Tattooist of Auschwitz* is Lale's story—Lale's and Gita's.

On the next page, I'm including just three of the countless entries I made on that spreadsheet. They record my first meeting, one other, and my very last.

A Writer's Journey with a Holocaust Survivor

	My Story		Lale's Story	
Date	Where, what I did/said	What I felt	What he said	His emotion
12/3/03	First meet Lale, his doggies, bad coffee and wafer biscuits.	What am I hearing? What have I got here?	Names, names, Gita, Baretski, Hoess. Hurry up and write! I need to be with Gita.	Grieving terribly. Abrupt, impatient, agitated.
	Acknowledge my ignorance of Judaism and the Holocaust.	Embarrassed. Ashamed.	A good thing. You will bring no preconceptions or baggage to hearing my story.	Seemed mildly amused.
	Own up to my German ancestors.	Frustration at not being able to connect, follow the disjointed rambling stories being shot at me.	No problem. We can't choose our parents.	Nonplussed.
04/04/04	Meet at his apartment. Still bad coffee, still like the wafer biscuits.	Weighed down with unbearable feelings of horror and sadness at what he and Gita went through. Don't know what to do with these feelings, which seem to be being transferred from Lale to me.	Has changed since meeting my family and telling me his doggies like me. He likes me, I can tell his story.	Lale opening up more. Says it feels good to get what to him have been not only stories but secrets about him and Gita in camp out to someone else. His enduring love for Gita always there, in the room with us.

My Story			Lale's Story	
Date	Where, what I did/said	What I felt	What he said	His emotion
10/31/05	The Alfred Hospital. Gary has told doctors he would like me to see Lale, who will probably not last the night—he has suffered a stroke.	Shattered.	He is no longer conscious, at first a little agitated, but as I hold his hand and whisper to him he seems to settle. It is time for me to say goodbye to him.	

I will never forget my last meeting with Lale. Gary contacted me to say that Lale was in the hospital, and that I should come and see him. I went as soon as I could, and sat with him for about an hour. He was no longer conscious, but at one point he seemed to become a little agitated, muttering something. I settled him, whispering to him, holding his hand, kissing him on the cheek. I remember saying to him, "If you want to join Gita, I'm sure Gary will understand. Go, be with her, and thank you for three wonderful years. I will never, ever stop trying to tell your story."

As I sat talking to Lale, holding his hand, we were interrupted by a doctor and nurse who told me they needed to tend to him, so it was time for me to leave. As I stood up to go, I said to them, "Please take good care of him. He is someone so special; this man is living history." The doctor responded, "We take care of all our patients." It was a silly thing for me to say—I knew he would be getting the best of care, but still, I said it.

The nurse walked around to the other side of the bed, looking at the hand I was holding. She said, "I saw the numbers on his arm." The doctor, obviously seeing Lale for the first time, asked, "What numbers?" The nurse said to him softly, "He is a Holocaust survivor." I found myself telling them a little about who Lale was, how he had been the Tattooist in Auschwitz and that was where he met the love of his life. The nurse held Lale's other hand and didn't even try to hide the tears that ran down her cheeks. I looked at the young doctor and he was frozen, staring at Lale, not saying a word. I had to be the one to say I would go and let them take care of him. The nurse came around the bed to me and hugged me tightly, the doctor took my hand and thanked me for telling him about his patient.

Lale died a few hours later with his son Gary by his side. I remain forever indebted to Gary for allowing me to spend time with Lale before he joined Gita.

Making Yourself Vulnerable

The renowned American research professor of social work Dr. Brené Brown describes vulnerability as our ability to make human connections by empathy, belonging, and loving. I would like to add, and by allowing ourselves to be loved, by accepting that we are worthy of love and connection.

How easy is it to build a wall around your heart and only allow your head to rule? All too easy. It's the safe option when first meeting someone. If there is no intention of connecting with the person emotionally, it makes sense to reveal very little about yourself, to move on. When an ongoing relationship begins to form, how quickly and how much of ourselves we reveal becomes a personal decision. This is where it gets tricky. Can you reasonably expect someone to open up, make themselves vulnerable to you if you don't return the favor?

Lale wanted to tell someone his story, this we both knew. He was telling me his story piecemeal, disjointed, with limited connection and coherency from one story to another. He was saying that I had to write his story, but he wasn't really telling it, not yet. I was struggling to understand what he wanted, whether he really wanted to speak about the past. When he did talk about his time in Auschwitz, his voice was often strangely clinical and devoid of emotion. The only time he seemed to lose control was when he spoke about Gita. Many times, he would start to say something, pause, and look away or call one of his doggies to come so he could pat her, calm himself, and switch to talking about something else.

Then one day as we sat there, with him, as so often, circling the story, touching upon it, and then quickly darting away, something occurred to me: Lale seemed comfortable talking with me, welcomed me warmly, was indignant if he felt too long had gone between visits. But he was the one doing all the talking and now our meetings had taken on a strangely artificial feeling. It was as though we were stuck in the lobby, twiddling our thumbs, waiting for something to begin. He'd asked me very little about myself and I had responded very blandly to his questions—I'd told him the names of my husband and children, told him about my work. The most intimate detail I'd given him was my mother's maiden name, back on the first day we'd met. No personal details had flowed from me to him. And looking back, I realize that when he had asked, I'd shied away from volunteering more than the most basic of details—he'd asked a little, but I'd clammed up in response. It wasn't that I was keeping anything from him, but in hindsight, I had misread his insistence on needing to tell his story quickly so he could be with Gita as a lack of interest in anything else. I had managed to create an atmosphere when we were together that gave him a sense of safety. He was definitely comfortable with me—he both greeted and farewelled me with a kiss on both cheeks, insisting I tell him when I would next return. But something was missing in our connection and it occurred to me that I was partly to blame for this.

Things changed after I took Lale home and introduced him to my family. Once that had happened, before he had even shut his door behind us on my arrival, he was asking after my daughter. Occasionally, he asked about the men in my life, but always my daughter. Something had changed between us— there was a warmth, an openness now. A week or two after our family dinner, we made the final breakthrough in his trusting me to hear and tell his story. By making myself vulnerable and letting Lale meet my family and learn some home truths about who I was, my good and bad points, I had enabled a much closer connection between us. Generally, I protect my family from all but our closest friends, but I let Lale in. I let him see me through their eyes without a filter. While he would need time to process what he learned about me, at least he now had something to process.

With the connection between our two families, a new level of trust was established between us. It was as if a light switch had been flicked. Lale now began to talk about the evil and horror he had experienced and witnessed in a deeply emotional manner, often openly weeping with me; telling me of the pain he felt at the atrocities he saw, his struggle to stay optimistic with Gita. Having heard him talk with my family about his time before and after Auschwitz, I would steer him toward happier memories when I could see him really struggling.

One day, I showed up to see him and decided that this time I needed a decent cup of coffee. When he opened the door—he was now always waiting with the door open as I walked up the steps to his apartment—I greeted him with, "Can we go out for coffee?"

He jumped at the suggestion, checked his pocket for his wallet, and grabbed his car keys. This was the first—and last—time I let Lale drive me. His doing a U-turn in the street without looking in any direction had me closing my eyes and saying goodbye to my family. Thankfully, we only drove a short distance to a nearby café, but all road rules were ignored. I didn't know whether to laugh or cry when he pulled into a nonstanding zone, killed the engine, and got out of the car. Scrambling behind him, I pointed out he couldn't park where he was leaving the car. With a flick of his hand, he told me he always parked there, nobody else did. I didn't bother trying to explain to him there was a reason for that.

When we walked into the small café, which had clearly remained unchanged for decades, every customer and all the staff called out Lale's name. The women all came rushing over to embrace him and receive his customary kiss on each cheek. I got my decent cup of coffee, but what I enjoyed more was seeing Lale come alive around people he knew well and accept their condolences; the women all asking if he was eating well and commenting on how he had lost weight. I was welcomed into their circle and the questions flew at me about what I was doing with Lale.

I hoped this excursion would be the start of Lale reconnecting with the Jewish community I knew he and Gita had been such a part of. Gita had died five months earlier. He had shown me many photos of the two of them out socializing. Quite the social butterflies they were: Lale always immaculate, Gita looking stunning. Often in the photos Lale was not looking down the lens like Gita was, but staring with so much love at the woman beside him.

A few weeks later, he asked me if I would go out with him to that first social event, mentioned earlier.

It was being held in the function room above the Jewish Holocaust Centre in Melbourne. I recognized this as an essential step in Lale introducing me to his world: he wanted me to hear from his friends about him. He too was now making himself vulnerable in order to cement our relationship. I would be there to provide moral support, should he feel the need to leave early, and there was no doubt he wanted his friends to know he was going to have his story told and to show them the person who was going to tell it. He wore this like a badge of honor when introducing me to friends and acquaintances alike.

Dressed up from my usual attire of jeans and a T-shirt, I knocked on his apartment door. He greeted me dressed in a perfectly ironed shirt, pants, and jacket, looking oh so dapper. I took his proffered arm and we walked to my car. He knew I would be driving but played the gentleman and opened the driver's door for me.

Parking wasn't the easiest in the quiet little street where the center is located. I offered to drop him off and go and find a space, but he wouldn't hear of it—he was perfectly capable of walking whatever distance was required.

Walking up the stairs to the function room, I guessed

from the noise level that we were entering an already crowded room. I later found out from Lale that he had told me the event started half an hour later than it did as he wanted everyone else to be there when we made our entrance.

We took two steps inside the room then he stopped. Someone saw him, called out his name and a chorus of "Lale! Lale's back!" went up around the room. Like an actor onstage at the end of a performance, he bowed deeply with the biggest smile I had ever seen on him. Lale, the playboy, was back.

I was hugely grateful to be swallowed up by dozens of very well-dressed and bejeweled ladies, all talking at once, wanting to know who I was and what I was doing with Lale. As I stumbled to find the words to explain my presence, I looked over at him surrounded by his friends, but he was watching me, making sure that I was OK. As I shook my head at him, half smiling, half scowling, he blew me a kiss and turned away, back to the conversation going on around him.

I looked at the women surrounding me, at the men on the other side of the room. I lowered the mean age of those in attendance by quite a few years. Men and women in their seventies, eighties, and nineties, dressed in beautiful tailored clothes; many of the men in suits with shiny shoes. Waitstaff moved between them all, some carrying trays with drinks, others food. The men were just as loud and animated as the women around me. Such a lovely scene, I felt honored to be part of it. Several times I heard one of the men say, "She not Jewish?" Lale would snap back, "No, I told you, I don't want someone Jewish writing my book." The conversations continued, but I could hear them circling back to: "No part of her Jewish, are you sure she isn't?"

I tried to explain what I was doing there, while slurping wine and dropping crumbs on the floor, always another glass, another pastry held out to me. It seemed important I accept a drink or food from every woman present in order to be connected to them, individually and collectively.

I wasn't sure what to expect when I told them I was spending time with Lale so I could write about his and Gita's life in Auschwitz-Birkenau. What I got was overwhelming support and encouragement. All of them piled in, wanting to tell me about their friendship with the couple. Each woman I met seemed to be trying to outdo the other, claiming their friendship was the longest, the deepest. I can't remember how many times I heard the words, "Did you know Gita . . ."

As all these stories of Lale and Gita were being relayed, shouted at me, I realized I had found my fount of knowledge of all things about Gita through her relationship with her female friends. These were stories Lale either didn't know or didn't consider important, as many of them didn't involve him. They told me what a wonderful cook Gita was. Lale never mentioned her cooking or baking anything. It was lovely to hear how proud she was of her "table" when Shabbat dinner was held at their place. Many of them were envious of the beautiful clothes Gita wore, particularly as she made them herself. I had seen many photos of her looking stunning, in perfectly fitted dresses. "Yes, she made them herself," I was told. Later, Lale confirmed she made her own clothes, designed them too. When I asked him about her being a good cook, he responded he just ate what he was given and never thought about it. The fact he'd never been interested in food when I mentioned it in the past made sense now.

When I asked the women whether they knew what Gita's time in Birkenau would have been like for her, they exchanged puzzled looks and shrugged their shoulders. "Of course we know what it was like for her," they said. "We were there, too." I felt so small—how could I not have asked this question sooner?

I was amazed at how freely they talked about their experiences during the Holocaust. Lale had told me many times how Gita would never talk about her time in Auschwitz; I had assumed from this that other female Holocaust survivors would not want to talk about it either. Here, I was hearing about it for the first time from a female perspective. What stood out for me was the constant reference to the cold. Lale mentioned the weather but only when referring to it being summer or winter. It seemed the overriding memory these women had was of being so bitterly cold, they didn't know how they survived.

I listened as one woman would say to another, "How would you know what it was like? You were only there for a week! I was there for years." Or, "You were not in Auschwitz. We had the worst camp, yours was a holiday camp compared to it." To me as an outsider it sounded like they were bickering before I realized this was the way they spoke to each other and no one was taking offense at being corrected or criticized. When one woman told me that she had a story like Lale and Gita's and would I write about it too, I was flooded by requests to "Write my story, tell my story!"

For several hours, I was part of this incredible group of women survivors, listening to anecdotes of enormous personal suffering, peppered with small, joyous moments. There were times when after a woman had told a short anecdote, her friends would say to her, "I didn't know that, you've not told us about that before." The shrug of shoulders was often followed by, "Well, I didn't want to talk about it before, now I do and maybe she," indicating me, "might want to tell my story too."

I have seen it in movies, read about it in books, but hearing one woman describe being separated from her parents and younger siblings at selection is an entirely different matter. Several women gave her a hug—they clearly knew the story but still responded with physical affection and so I took her hand, looked into her eyes, letting them say all that I couldn't. With her other hand, she stroked my face and smiled back at me. A small connection between two strangers, remembered by me. The physical pain I felt in my chest stayed with me for quite a while.

When Lale finally wandered over and said he wanted to leave, I didn't want to go. Names and phone numbers were being scribbled on tissues, pieces of paper found in handbags and thrust at me with a "Call me." I subsequently met with many of these women on many, many other occasions. I am sure they worked out that I was only going to tell Lale and Gita's story, but whenever we were together, it was almost as if I was a facilitator, helping them to talk among themselves, compare notes and experiences, to speak openly about the trauma of the past, their guilt and shame at having survived. Under the guise of talking to me, an outsider, they somehow felt they had permission to open up about this terrible time in their lives. I was humbled by this. It was a huge privilege to be included in this tight-knit group with a shared experience and to hear stories they had often not related to anyone before, not even to their own families.

How much children of survivors know of their parents' experiences seems to vary greatly. I have met children who know every detail of their parents' time during the Holocaust, but the majority of children of survivors tell me they know very little of this time. Many say it is because their mother or father told them in no uncertain terms that they did not want to talk about it. Others told me they were too afraid to ask, anxious about causing upset and worried how they themselves would cope with the knowledge of the horror and evil their beloved parent had experienced. I have been asked countless times for advice on how to get a survivor to talk to their children and if I would be prepared to meet them and listen to their story. If there is one thing I have learned from speaking to survivors, it is that they will only ever tell you something they want you to know, you cannot force them to talk. I have suggested finding someone who has no emotional connection to the survivor for them to talk to may help them to open up, but there is no guarantee.

* * *

As our friendship deepened, Lale invited me into his world more and more often. Sometimes he took me to a smaller coffee catch-up with his male friends. Several of these men would talk to me about their Holocaust experiences, acknowledging that they were survivors, but never at an emotional level, mostly saying nothing, just nodding their heads in a knowing, "I was there" way. I met one of Lale's closest friends several times, went to his home, met his wife.

Tuli was only seventeen when he was taken away. He was also from Slovakia, from Bardejov, a small town I have visited—the same town Cilka Klein came from. He was only in Birkenau a few months before being sent to another work camp, but he did tell me of the extreme hunger he suffered while there. This appears to be his overriding memory: starvation.

A quietly spoken man, Tuli seemed the opposite to Lale in personality. Where Lale would say the first thing that came to mind, Tuli was reserved and considered in everything he said in my company. In the company of his male friends, Lale loved to tell them about me and my family—and yes, my daughter in particular. This would generate conversation among the men, all wanting to know more about who I was, where I came from—I really loved the fact that Lale seemed proud to have me as a friend.

I felt so safe opening up and talking about who I was, telling stories of my life growing up in rural New Zealand, and they seemed genuinely interested. And I came to realize that it was when I talked at a personal level about myself that the men would be more forthcoming about themselves and their families, both their immediate families in Australia but also, gradually, those they had lost. It was clear the loss of their families during the Holocaust was the most significant thing they wanted to tell me. It was as if what evil and horror they had seen and had inflicted on them paled in comparison to the deaths of members of their family. Was this survivor guilt being expressed? What I do know is what I heard. No pain inflicted on them compared to the pain of living full lives when their parents, siblings, had perished.

When I think about my time with Lale and listening to him, several stories jump out at me as being emotionally draining for him to tell and for me to hear. One in particular I remember so vividly and still get upset thinking about it. This was the day he told me about returning to his home town of Krompachy and finding his sister Goldie alive. The mixed emotion of finding one surviving family member and learning that the rest of his family had been taken and probably wouldn't be returning was visceral, physically painful for him, even when talking about it six decades later. Hearing it, I felt the same way. I asked the men if it helped that they had married and had children of their own, formed their own families. Everyone to whom I asked this question told me it didn't help at all: the two things were separate, one could not balance out the other, replace the other.

I started this chapter asking if listening was simple. I do believe it can be. You won't always feel you got it right, or that a conversation went well—I certainly don't. Tell yourself that as long as you did your best, on the day, given whatever circumstances were conspiring against you or supporting you, then that was good enough. There are, however, a few steps to making it simple. Being an active listener is not something you have to remind yourself to do. Whether talking to your nearest and dearest, your elders, children, the process is the same. Like all things in life, we don't always follow the processes needed for the outcome we desire. It all comes down to making the decision to be vulnerable and letting others see that. Why should someone trust you with their hopes and fears, their past and dreams for the future, if they don't feel it will be reciprocated? The answer is simple: they won't. I listened with apprehension and joy to my children "telling tales" about me to Lale. They didn't hold back. The first day they met him, he gathered them into his circle, shared with them aspects of his past. He made himself vulnerable to them, they responded, secure in the knowledge that what they said about their mother would be respected and enjoyed. They gave him ammunition to fire back at me when he was in a playful mood, which was often. By letting Lale into my family, we created a world for me to listen and him to tell me a story he was desperate to share.

The day after Lale died, my family joined me in attending his funeral service and burial and that evening, we entered a synagogue for the first time in order to say farewell to him. He was gone now to be with Gita, but he will never be forgotten by any of us.

Going the Extra Mile

"I've run out of clean knickers," I told my publisher in London from my hotel room in Johannesburg, where I was doing publicity for my novels *The Tattooist of Auschwitz* and *Cilka's Journey*. I was due to return home in two days' time, but I had made the phone call that would change everything. The phone call to Rehovot, Israel, where I had spoken to a ninety-two-year-old lady named Livia. Listened as she told me the story of being taken from Slovakia in March 1942, along with her eldest sister. Listened as she told me she remembered Lale Sokolov making the number on her left arm as she entered Auschwitz-Birkenau. Listened as she told me she and her two sisters moved to Israel after the war. Listened as she asked me to come to Israel to see her, to hear her story. I then spoke to her son, whose email had kept me awake a few days earlier: "I think my mum and her sisters have a story you might like to hear," he had written. He was right.

"Buy some new knickers," I was told. My publisher sensed what I was sensing. This was a story worth going that extra mile for—five thousand miles in fact.

I checked the address Livia had given me— Rehovot was a town just inland from Tel Aviv—and went looking for accommodation nearby. From what I could see, it was a satellite town of Tel Aviv; hotel accommodation was in short supply. I checked with airlines to determine if it was possible to fly from Johannesburg to Tel Aviv. Yes, it was. I phoned home and asked my family how they felt about me staying away another week, as I had somewhere I needed to go. *Then go you must*, I was told—they didn't ask for more details.

Two hours after I was due to fly from Johannesburg to Melbourne, I flew to Tel Aviv. An overnight flight that had me land early in the morning, alone in a country I had never visited before, where I did not speak the language, but with new knickers in my bag. I hadn't obtained any local currency but hey, credit cards work everywhere, don't they? I had managed to make a booking at the nearest hotel to where Livia lived and asked the taxi driver to take me there. We skirted around the city of Tel Aviv and made our way to Rehovot. It was the middle of summer and even early in the morning, a heat haze rose from the ground and bounced off the buildings as I passed by.

Pulling up outside the hotel, I handed over my card.

"No card, only cash," came a firm rebuke.

When I explained, or tried to explain, that I had just arrived in the country and hadn't got any cash, the driver took off, away from the hotel, with me still prisoner in his back seat. Mild panic as I calmly asked where we were going. It would appear the letters ATM are used in many languages and I understood I was being taken to one, where I would get cash, and only then would I be returned to the hotel.

At an ATM, freestanding on the side of a dirt road, no obvious connection to any building, let alone a bank, I grudgingly left the taxi, my bags still inside, and handed over my card to a machine whose written instructions for use I could not read. With no idea of the exchange rate, having been told how many shekels were required, I guessed which buttons to push and doubled the amount I was being asked to pay the taxi driver.

My card was spat back out at me, shekels followed.

When I had booked the hotel room, I paid for an extra day so I could get into a room early in the morning. A shower was sorely needed. I had been told by Livia's son to come to their address as soon as I could. Within the hour, I was back in a taxi. I offered my card, ever hopeful, only to be told cash-only. One step ahead of this taxi driver, I offered up the cash. The note I handed over was thrust back at me as being too big—the driver wanted the correct amount or something close to it. My explanation that the ATM only gave me large notes wasn't accepted. I was then told I would be driven to a shop where I could buy something and get some small change.

Welcome to Israel.

The taxi eventually left me outside an apartment building. As I got out, I looked up to see Livia, her son and daughter-in-law waving from the first-floor balcony. As I made it to the building entrance, the door opened and Livia's son greeted me with the warmest hug and ushered me upstairs to the waiting arms of his mother and wife. What a welcome! This was the introduction to Israel I will remember.

"You must be hungry. Sit down, we have breakfast ready for you, and coffee, surely you must need coffee?"

It was not yet 9 a.m.

I spent two days with Livia, meeting other members of her family, listening to them tell the story of the three sisters from Slovakia who'd survived Auschwitz-Birkenau. No one held back—they wanted me to hear as much as they could get out in the brief time I had in Israel. Knowing I would not have the time I'd had with Lale to hear Livia's story, and knowing once again I did not want the distraction of writing notes, I asked Livia's daughter-in-law if she would make notes for me. And as I had done so often in my life, and as I had done especially with my dear friend Lale, I sat and listened. And drank strong Turkish coffee and ate something new every hour, on the hour. This time, however, the coffee was wonderful—I was going back for seconds!

In the initial email I received from Livia's son and daughter-in-law, they had told me that Livia came from the same town as Gita. They told me her number was 4559, three after Gita's. Livia had not slept, they reported, as she read *The Tattooist of Auschwitz*—she was astounded and couldn't believe how accurate my writing was. They also told me Livia remembered incidents with Gita as she was with her often and would like to provide me with details in support of some of the parts of my book that had received criticism. Livia had an incredible memory, they said, and wanted to set the record straight, face-to-face.

The phone call that followed two days after that first email was extremely emotional, with all of us crying at certain moments. Livia's son told me how, when his mother saw the Australian book jacket (which shows two numbered arms), she simply said, "That must be about Lale and Gita." *Wow, what a thing to hear!* It was while talking to Livia, when she said very clearly that she wanted to see me, not talk over the phone, that I knew I had to go to her—I too prefer to talk face-to-face.

As I hung up, I realized I was shaking. I was covered in goose bumps too. I needed to go to see Livia and her family immediately. Making a phone call to my publishers in London, I needed only a few minutes of talking with them before I was told, "Get on that plane."

After only a five-minute phone conversation, I knew I had to follow my instinct. I had listened to the beautiful voice of an elderly woman. I did not judge or question why her family had contacted me, Livia speaking to me—it just felt right. I thought back to that cup of coffee I had had with a friend all those years ago, who told me about a man who might have a story worth telling, and I felt the same way.

This was something I needed to do—it just felt right.

In this instance, time and circumstance and experience and those encouraging words from my publisher meant that I took going the extra mile to extremes. But I also "went the extra mile" that first time I agreed to have a cup of coffee with an old man who was grieving over the death of his wife. And even more simply than that, by going the extra mile, I mean being open as a listener. When we listen actively, the aim is not to judge, not to form an "opinion" about what we are being told. Equally, and we should all practice this more, we should aim to listen without attempting to think of a response—doing so is almost a distraction in itself. We don't need to comment on everything we are told. In fact, in many cases, it is probably better not to say anything than risk saying the wrong thing.

With Lale and with Livia, as I've said, I didn't want to do anything that would distract me from what I was there to hear, or that would distract either of them from what they wanted to say. So I didn't take notes, although I did later record Livia and myself speaking together. This process of really listening and being open involves not only hearing the words, but also listening to the silences in between and the context in which they are being spoken. Like Lale, Livia reached out to me via her son, because she is old and wants her and her sisters' extraordinary story told while there is still time. What I knew to do from my experience with Lale was to present myself to her—make myself vulnerable in the sense of pitching up slightly bleary-eyed, alone, fresh off a plane—and try to show her quickly who I am and what I stand for just by being present in the moment. I tried to put aside all thoughts of whether this was a story I could work with, whether she really would decide to tell me all, where the story was leading, and simply listen, be there open before her, ready to hear her. The story she had to tell me was one of enormous power, hope, survival, courage, and one of love. And being allowed to listen to Livia, to meet her ninety-four-year-old sister Magda and her beautiful extended family, has been one of the greatest privileges of my life. Livia's eldest sister, Cibi, died in 2014.

As my second day with Livia and her family was ending, Livia told me I should take tomorrow off and go up to Jerusalem. My ignorance of geography was shown up when I said I couldn't possibly travel there and back in a day. You have to remember, I come from Australia, where to go from one city to another generally requires an airplane. Thankfully, Livia's son and daughter-in-law live in Canada and know the perils of distance in getting around a country. The next day, a driver took me the forty minutes "up the road" to Jerusalem. I asked him to take me directly to Yad Vashem—The World Holocaust Remembrance Center. If I was going to be in Jerusalem, I wanted that to be my first stop. For five hours, I wandered around this amazing museum. I spent time in their archive area with a very kind assistant helping me look up databases to see what information they held on Lale, Gita, and Cilka. Before I left, I went into the shop there. Seeing *The Tattooist of Auschwitz* prominently displayed was a shock. I'm not sure why, but I wasn't expecting to see the English version there. I knew the rights to translate the story into Hebrew had been sold into Israel, but my understanding was that it hadn't been released yet.

I picked up a copy and was looking at it, overcome

to have it in my hands in this most holy of holiest places dedicated to the Holocaust. A shop assistant approached and asked me if I wanted to buy it. I blurted out that I was the author, this was my book, and I thanked her for having it here. She called over her manager and in a lengthy conversation I was told how well the book sold there, how they were always having to ask the supplier for more copies. Then I was told that many people had come into their shop asking for the book, describing the country they had come from and how they wanted to read this story, but more importantly, how they wanted to buy it here, at Yad Vashem.

I come from a small rural town in New Zealand. I am well into my sixties and here I was at Yad Vashem in Jerusalem, being told readers came from around the world to this place to buy my book. I bought a copy—I too wanted to own a copy of *The Tattooist of Auschwitz* bought at Yad Vashem.

It was getting late in the afternoon when I left the shop to have a cup of coffee in the café there. Backstory. While I was in Johannesburg, what now seemed like a long time ago, but in fact was only a few days, a woman approached me after hearing me speak at an event. We chatted and she asked me where I was going from there. I told her I might go to Israel. She said she had a good friend who lived in Jerusalem and if I made it there, I should contact him. She had subsequently sent him a message saying she had met me, and I might be in touch. While drinking the coffee, I flicked through my phone and saw a message from the man, saying if I was in Jerusalem to give him a call. Acting on impulse, I called him. He was working for another few hours, but he invited me to have dinner with him and his wife. At this point she knew nothing about me and most definitely did not know she would be cooking for a stranger that evening. He suggested I get myself up to the Old City and explore. He would call me in a few hours and arrange to meet up and take me home.

Trusting, aren't I? Don't tell my family!

Exploring the Old City was wonderful. Such a colorful, alive area, bustling with people, old and young. I wandered up and down the cobblestone streets buying the occasional souvenir, sampling the local food. At an arranged street corner, a car pulled up and a stranger said, "Get in." I did as I was told.

We drove to his home where his wife had cooked an amazing meal for the three of us. We ate outside on their balcony with stunning views over the city as the sun set on my third day in Israel. We talked for hours. After midnight, my new friend drove me all the way back to my hotel. From him and his wife I was given a lesson in the politics and history of Israel. At university, I had studied the Arab-Israeli conflict. Thought I knew all about it—I knew nothing. Now I know more. What an honor to spend an evening with locals prepared to share stories of their life in a country still racked by conflict. All they want is for the clashes to end. They were practicing living in peace with Palestinians, choosing an apartment building largely inhabited by their friends, people of Palestine.

The next day, I went back to Livia and her family, spending another three days with them. Listening, primarily, but also telling them something of myself as they wanted to know about my family too. My phone was produced on more than one occasion as three generations of Livia's and her sister's families came to meet me and I proudly showed off photos of my grandchildren (the adults not so much!).

It transpired that the day I went up to Jerusalem, members of the three sisters' families had gathered to talk about me, share their opinions on whether I could be trusted to tell their story. Apparently, I was considered more than acceptable and toward the end of my stay, a formal request to "tell the story of the three sisters from Slovakia" was made to me. This extraordinary tale of hope, love, and survival became the subject of my next novel.

A week late, I returned home to share with my family and publishers snippets of what I had learned, what I had heard, and the rich experience that had come out of being prepared to go the extra mile.

* * *

A few years ago, I made another journey. The geography was closer to Australia, the destination a world away from anywhere I had been before or since.

Timor-Leste.

For several years I had been associated in a small way with one of the most inspirational, amazingly generous people I have ever met. Several times a year this man travels to Timor-Leste, bringing to that impoverished country his expertise as a brilliant cardiologist. There, he identified young boys and girls whose life expectancy was limited if they did not receive a simple cardiac procedure that is carried out all day, every day, in Western countries. Once identified, he used his resources to bring these children to Australia for life-saving procedures, carried out by equally gifted and compassionate doctors at major public hospitals. I had a small role in helping to care for these patients, and their caregivers and translators, when they came to the hospital where I worked. These were some of the most rewarding interactions I experienced in my twenty years working in the social work department of a major hospital.

I was asked to accompany a small team going to Dili, the capital city of Timor-Leste, to see a new round of patients and check on those who had been lucky enough to have been treated by this wonderful cardiologist, who gave them back their lives. Also on this trip was the cardiologist's wife, who had made the journey many times with her husband and who had been instrumental in assisting remote communities in both bringing fresh water to the many smaller villages that existed in the Highlands outside of Dili and also in the development and creation of a school.

With no medical expertise to offer, I accompanied the cardiologist's wife on a two-day journey up the mountain to visit the school she had been involved with and see the bamboo pipeline running down the side of the road—no, more just a track—bringing fresh water to the villages. We were being driven by a local man who was to be our guide and translator: his name was Eddie.

I sat in the front of a four-wheel drive with Eddie on the six hours it took us to travel some seventy kilometers up a mountain. The path was nonexistent in many places. Several times, Eddie got out of the vehicle to study the track and the distance from the side of the cliff to the drop-off to calculate if we could make it. I doubt if we went over ten kilometers an hour at any time in the drive to our destination.

Eddie had a very distinctive vehicle and it turned out everyone along that narrow track, in every village we passed through, knew who drove it. As we approached the first village, I looked in awe as men and women, boys and girls, ran out from their homes, barely four walls, some with roofs, many without, calling out his name, waving their arms in greeting, in homage. With his window wound down, Eddie waved back as they ran alongside the vehicle and often stopped, got out, and chatted with some of the men for a few minutes before resuming our journey.

My traveling companion explained to me that Eddie is almost godlike to everyone in this small country. He is the most revered person she has ever known. Often when Eddie stopped, the two of us got out and played with the children, who giggled, pulled at our clothing, and showed off their skills in throwing a stone or a stick. Toddlers stumbled around naked. No diapers here. The women hung back, shy, giggling, wondering who we were. When we waved and called out hello to them, they waved back.

I had been told a little bit about Eddie, this remarkable man who fled his homeland as a young boy. Timor-Leste was invaded in 1975 by Indonesia and over several years, 50 percent of the country was killed or died from disease. During those terrible times, Eddie lived in Australia and was educated there, but he returned to his country in 1999 when the United Nations took control. Since then, he has worked tirelessly toward providing healthcare and education for all. Refusing any political alliance, he has remained independent of all the factions still scrambling to govern one of the youngest countries in our region. In doing so, he has earned the respect of everyone.

As we drove up into the mountains I asked a few casual questions of Eddie, wanting to understand a little about how his country was coping, wanting to hear from him the history that had the three of us now traveling together to see a small school buried deep in the jungle. I made it clear to him that I was open to hearing his story, if he wanted someone to listen to him.

He answered my gentle questions, then slowly started offering insights without prompts. Over the next two days I heard the most amazing stories as this humble man shared the joy and hope he had for the country of his birth. The country where his brother died back in 1975, fighting the invading Indonesian Army, and to which he was the only member of his family who had returned.

On our return to Dili, I asked if I could talk further with him and possibly write his story. He said no. I was told he had been approached by many journalists and writers, from Australia and the United States, who wanted to tell his story. He always refused—he considered he was just one person doing all he could to help the people of Timor-Leste have a better life. What I can tell you is that he is no ordinary man, living in an extraordinary time and place: he is an *extraordinary* man making a huge difference. Over the next few days, while I remained in his country, we spoke often. He introduced me to his wife, showed me pictures of his young children.

Eddie makes a huge difference to his community, a community in desperate need. However, we can all make a difference wherever we are. It can be as simple as checking on an elderly neighbor, volunteering to serve your community in a small way, or listening to someone who wants to talk to you. There were many times at the hospital when I was involved with parents following the death of their baby that I felt totally hopeless—there was nothing I could say to ease the gut-wrenching pain reflected on their faces. But I would get a heartfelt "thank you" for helping to organize their child's funeral and I knew that just doing one simple, practical thing can make a difference, even a very small one.

Twelve months later, my friend the cardiologist was back in Dili, doing what he does best: trying to save young lives. As always, Eddie was his driver and translator. I got an email from my friend while he was there. There was no message, just the subject line: *Eddie says yes.* I hope one day I will have the opportunity to return to Timor-Leste and find a way to tell the story of Eddie, the bravest person I have ever met. Eddie has definitely gone the extra mile in returning to his country when he could so easily have remained and lived a good life in Australia. He has faced physical dangers in confronting enemies in a country still torn by conflict and struggling to find its identity. I will, when I can, go the extra mile and return to Dili and hopefully, proudly, tell Eddie's story.

Experience has shown me time and again that if I take myself somewhere, out of my comfort zone, with an open mind, I will find someone with an amazing story to tell.

All I have to do is listen.

Asking the Right Question

I'm often asked, how does the listener know what is the right question at the right moment, what do people want to be asked, or what question will unlock a story? How do we sense what is a gentle prompt, an indicator that we're prepared to listen, and what might instead be intrusive?

When I consider these questions, I always hear the words Lale said to me when we first met. He asked the question, "Did you know I was the *Tätowierer*?" I had to say no on two counts. I had just met him, and I did not know what his story was, and I had no idea what a *Tätowierer* was. He replied, "Well, I was, I was the person making the numbers on the arms at Auschwitz-Birkenau." He pulled up his shirt sleeve and placed his left arm inches from my face. I kept my expression neutral as my eyes followed the fading green numbers he was pointing to: 32407. I now knew what a *Tätowierer* was.

I knew the key to learning Lale's story was to listen, not interrupt. The few times I asked a question midsentence, he would get cranky, lose his way in the story he was telling, and struggle to reconnect. Instead, I had to work with his broken story lines, fired at me often at bullet pace, with limited or no connection from one to the other. As you can imagine, with so many disjointed facts, emotional and clinical, there had to come a time when I needed to ask questions, get clarification—a deeper understanding of what he had witnessed and experienced.

The day Lale said, "Have I told you about Cilka?" has become a watershed moment for me. When I said, "No, who was she?" he responded with the simple statement: "She was the bravest person," wagging his finger, "not the bravest girl, the bravest person I ever met." He then became distressed and wouldn't talk anymore about her other than to say, "We couldn't save her."

I let the conversation end there, knowing I would

come back to Cilka when I felt the time was right. In fact, it would take several months for me to get any details about her and her role in Birkenau because Lale would always become distraught when he recounted what she had endured there and during her subsequent imprisonment in a Siberian Gulag.

On one visit with his friend Tuli, Lale mentioned that Tuli and Cilka had come from the same town, Bardejov. I immediately asked Tuli what he remembered about her. He told me he knew her in their hometown, knew what she was doing in Birkenau, and felt sorry for her. He was the first person who said to me that Cilka did "bad" things. When pressed, he said he only heard what she was doing. She was, however, kind to him and took a risk to get him warm clothing and a blanket the first winter when he nearly died from the cold. He credits her with saving his life.

Tuli's comment that Cilka did "bad" things prompted me to ask other survivors about her, particularly the women I was now spending time with when accompanying Lale. As with Tuli, I heard contradictory stories: Cilka was a "terrible girl," countered with "she was so young, so brave," "she helped so many people with extra food and clothing, using her position as a protected prisoner." I knew I had to do as instructed by Lale: "When you finish writing my story, you must tell Cilka's—the world needs to know about her."

For many months, I kept in my handbag a list of questions for Lale, waiting for the right moment. As I have said, I used my intuition while Lale talked, stopping him when he was growing distressed or exhaustion was setting in. At that point, I would deliberately interrupt with a question. Not about him, Gita, the Holocaust, their life after, but about something unrelated—more often than not about sports. Then, after we had discussed the sport of the day, I would casually pull the piece of paper from my handbag and look for a question that would align with what he had most recently been talking about. "You talked about such and such last time we were together, can you tell me more about . . ."

Asking Lale a question in this manner usually got him excited and he would elaborate enthusiastically. It showed him I had been listening to him, he told me. Timing, it was always about the timing when asking a deeply emotional question, particularly if it related to Gita and later, Cilka. Both had saved his life, he said, each in their own way. Gita, by allowing him to love her, Cilka by begging a favor of the man raping her: "Help Lale." There were many days when talking and asking about these two women was a no-go zone and I would stick to other stories of his life in the camp.

There were two other aspects of his time in Birkenau that were extremely painful for Lale to recall. It meant that I had to be extremely careful when our conversations touched on them and just as sensitive in raising questions about them. These were his relationship with the Roma families and with the man who became known as the "Angel of Death," Josef Mengele.

As I've described earlier, Lale had befriended the Roma men and women he called his new family during the time he shared the block with them. He had given them hope that they too might find a way to survive the horror they were living through and he then had to watch, with a rifle pointed at him and the threat to take him too, as all 4,500 Roma men, women, and children were loaded onto trucks in the dead of the night, only to rain down on him from the chimneys of the crematoria the next day. This was a deep trauma and guilt that I know he had lived with his entire life. Over many months I learned about this part of his story in Birkenau in small bursts of pain and anger. I feel there is much more to Lale's story here—he hinted at it enough times, but he chose to take it to his grave, and I respect that. And I certainly knew not to try and push him on it—it was never something I asked him about, I just listened when he found himself wanting to speak about it.

His stories about Mengele were different. Here, he had no trouble telling me of the evil and horror he saw perpetrated by that person, because his own feelings of guilt and shame were not so closely connected and also because he felt such a clear burning rage at what that man had done. He raged in anger at the extreme cruelty he witnessed, often against children.

Early on in my relationship with Lale, he took me to the Jewish Holocaust Centre in Melbourne, acting as my guide. He was quite calm, almost clinical, as he described and explained the exhibits. At one point he got a little ahead of me. I was alerted to his absence by his hysterical shouting and cursing. Along with others in the center, I rushed to his side as he collapsed, pointing, shaking, as he continued to curse the photo in front of him. It was Mengele, dressed in his doctor's white coat, taken in Auschwitz. Sixty years on, the terror he felt returned and he collapsed onto the floor. Remembering this remains painful for me to this day. I would subsequently hear from Lale much of what he had witnessed.

For the record, writing this part of Lale's story was the most difficult for me: what to leave out, what to put in. I experienced such horror myself in listening to the atrocities he described that after much deliberation, I decided to withhold much of what I heard. I did not want Lale's story to become Mengele's story.

Lale was in his late eighties when we first met (he died three days after we had sat eating cake and yes, drinking coffee, celebrating his ninetieth birthday) and he was dealing with memories that were often very painful, some of which he hadn't spoken about since the war ended. His memory was sharp, but he wasn't a natural storyteller. I had to draw his story together from his vignettes, from memories that came and went, and from the research I undertook when we weren't together. I spent hours reading about Auschwitz-Birkenau during the years that he was there and watching USC Shoah Foundation testimonies. The reading was often profoundly traumatic, shocking, upsetting, but picturing Lale, this dear old man who'd had such a rich life after the war ended, and the responsibility I felt to him, and to history, made it possible for me. Often, I would stumble across a story or detail in my research and raise it gently with him. Time and again he would surprise me by knowing exactly what I was referring to, jumping on it and fleshing out the bones of what was recorded in history books, bringing the story to life. If I ever asked why he had never mentioned it before, he would shrug and say it hadn't occurred to him, it hadn't seemed important, or that he hadn't thought about it for years. But he always knew what I was talking about, because he had been there, bearing witness to it all.

At one point I read about the time the Allies flew a plane low over Birkenau in spring 1944. I wanted to ask Lale whether he had been there, whether he remembered it happening, but I had to be very careful about bringing things up that he hadn't told me about—I was there to honor his story of the Holocaust, not the entire story of the Holocaust, and I was also very aware that there might be things he didn't touch on because they were too distressing. I saved the question for a time when we were talking about one of my sons leaving the country to go on an overseas trip. We talked about the size of the planes we now flew in and chatted generally about aircraft and what the Allies would have flown during

the war. Then I told him what I had read and asked
if he saw the plane, back in 1944. His reaction was
immediate: he jumped up from his chair and paced
around his living room, cursing. When I settled him
down and asked if he wanted to talk about it, he told
me he remembered it as clearly as if it had happened
yesterday.

On the first pass, in broad daylight, everyone who
was outside looked up as they thought the plane
was going to land on them—it was flying so low to
the ground. With a few others, Lale stood frozen to
the spot and watched it fly away, only to circle back
and make another low pass. Prisoners started moving about, he told me, walking aimlessly, looking up.
Lale was at the selection area, surrounded by SS, and
he was afraid of what their response to the aircraft
would be. He was numbering new arrivals and dared
not move, but he stopped briefly and watched as the
plane turned and headed back toward the camp. Hun-
dreds of prisoners acted as one, yelling and pointing
toward the crematoria, calling up into the sky: "Drop
the bombs, drop the bombs!" The plane passed low
one more time, then flew away. He went on to tell me
that every man and woman, boy and girl there that
day would have died happily in an attack by the Allies

if it meant destroying the gas chamber and cremato-ria. Instead, many perished as the SS opened fire on the shouting and waving prisoners.

Lale himself quickly moved to the nearby pro-cessing building, where prisoners were showered, shaved, and deloused, pressing himself hard against the structure. He stayed there until the shooting ceased and the surviving prisoners had fled to safety. A simple question about an event unlocked a memory that once again left me not knowing what to do with my distress and anger at what this beautiful old man had experienced. I had no hesitation about including this episode in my book, *The Tattooist of Auschwitz*. It was one of the rare vignettes I got from Lale in one go—I asked the right question, at the right moment and the story poured forth.

Another case of history and memory walking side by side. No parting.

As our relationship developed into friendship, I became more confident about asking Lale questions outright. I still picked my time and place carefully, depending on what I wanted to know and how sensi-tive the subject might be. For the most part, he was willing to answer all my questions, driven by the hope that in telling the world what he had experienced and witnessed, he was helping to ensure that the Holocaust would never happen again. He said this to me often: "You tell my story so it [the Holocaust] won't happen again." I would always respond in the same way: that I hoped I could tell his story appropriately, honoring the lives of the Jewish men, women, and children who had lived and been murdered during this terrible time.

When I look back on Lale's faith in me, it reminds me of the belief a child has in its parents that they will always do the right thing by them. That unconditional belief that comes when you fully trust someone. Lale seemed to fully trust that I would tell his story to a wide audience. *With or without Ryan Gosling.*

Listening to Lale was not always about hearing the words he said. Often it was what he *didn't* say, the silence in between the words. Often the expression of distress in his face, eyes watering, voice quavering, hands batting away demons and horror only he was seeing, told me more. It told me to leave things alone for the time being; to seek out the doggies to give him the physical contact he craved from them when distressed; to request another cup of coffee.

Practical Tips for Active Listening

Most of us can remember a time when we tried to share a confidence and our chosen listener turned away. It takes courage to reveal something personal, and to be met with indifference when you do can be devastating. Imagine how it feels to be a small child, offering something to a parent who is too busy to look, or an employee, bringing a problem to a boss who can't be bothered to engage.

A friend of mine, a senior manager with a lot on his plate, once told me how ashamed he'd felt when an anonymous survey among his staff revealed how hurt they were that he never seemed to raise his eyes from his screen when they came to talk to him. He claimed he actually *had* been listening to them (I don't think he can have been!), but he did accept that it was important that he was *seen* to be listening too. And I will never forget talking to Holocaust survivors at a large event celebrating the sixtieth anniversary of the liberation of Auschwitz. Lale took me there as his "escort." Security was intense as the Israeli Consul General was in attendance and a number of men and women mingling with over one thousand invited survivors and family, dressed in black suits, shirts and ties, had squiggly cords running from their ears into their jackets. They could frequently be seen talking into the cuffs of their shirts and the bulges under their jackets told me they were armed.

A crowd of Lale's friends gathered around us, all talking at once, caught up in the moment. I was acutely aware we were attracting the attention of security and out of the corner of my eye thought I saw several moving deliberately toward us. Distracted, I lost focus of the fact I had been asked a question. Lale tugged on my sleeve; everyone was looking at me: "You're not listening to us!" he exclaimed loudly. "Why aren't you listening?" I looked at the dozen or more faces staring at me. One of the women said quietly, "Lale says you always listen. Do you not want to hear what anyone else has to say?" I was mortified. Lale looked at me with disappointment. I apologized profusely, but the moment was gone.

Top Tips for Active Listening
Listening, *real* listening, is an active process. The active listener is aware of where and how they are sitting or standing, and what else is happening in the room. They are able to give full focus and by

controlling their own physical reactions to what is being shared, give the other person the space and the confidence to know they are being heard. Next time someone approaches you with something important to say, why not try the following?

- This might seem obvious, but if the other person is visiting you, make them welcome in your space. Pull out a chair, give them a cup of tea, clear papers off your desk if you are at work, turn your phone off or put it away. Do these things deliberately and obviously; you are setting a scene. If you are visiting them, let them take the lead in arranging your surroundings and wait until they are satisfied with them.
- Make sure you are on the same eye level, either sitting or standing. There's a reason why a good doctor will take a seat on the bed of a patient to give bad news.
- If you are in control of the environment, make sure they are not facing the light and that you do not have your back to it. For an open conversation, your face needs to be visible.
- Sometimes sitting facing each other can feel uncomfortable—a bit like prison visiting or the interrogation scenes familiar to us all from cop shows. Try sitting at ninety degrees rather than

opposite each other. Lale and I also sat at the table at ninety degrees, with me at the head, him at the seat next to me—his seating arrangement.

- Use the opening conversation to put the other person at ease and establish a connection. It can be the weather, the journey, a mutual friend, something general, but it serves to remind you both that you exist in the same human universe. During this time, you can also make sure that *you* are physically comfortable. Active listening involves being acutely aware of your own physical state.

- Try to keep your hands still—unless you are using an object to encourage a memory (see also page 49). Even then, you should turn it very slowly in your fingers rather than allow it to become a distraction.

- Once the other person has started talking, allow yourself to become completely quiet. Watch and listen for cues: How are they holding themselves? How are they speaking? Are they tensing up? Are they finding it difficult to get the words out? If it seems right, a nod or a quick smile, or a raise of the eyebrows will signal to them that you are following what they are saying and encourage them to continue.

- Resist the temptation to interrupt. Something they say may trigger a response and you may wish to chime in to validate what they are telling you by sharing a similar experience of your own. Hold back if you can—this is their moment.
- If they stall or dry up, it might be because they fear they have lost your attention for a moment, perhaps your eyes wandered by mistake or maybe they have reached the crucial and most sensitive part of their story and are hesitant to continue. Try repeating the last thing they said, or even back up a little and ask them for a detail from an earlier part of their story: "You never liked swimming..." or "You said you found your uncle very difficult, what day would you usually go over to visit?" Repeating what they have said confirms that you have been listening; asking for more detail from an earlier part of the story grounds it and allows them to go back and clarify, which may give a more secure base from which to move on.
- It's important to know when—and how—to help the teller *leave* a story. They may have told you as much as they can or want to and you need to respect that, even if the story is

unfinished. Make a mental note of the last thing they say and think about how you can pick it up again the next time you see them. I've spoken about the way Lale would sometimes stop abruptly and shake his head when the memories became too much to bear. I learned this was a signal to begin to bring our sessions to a close and I would start moving a little or lean over and pet one of his dogs to lower the intensity and give him space. After a moment, it would feel right to suggest the dogs needed an airing, or to ask him for his thoughts on whatever sport was playing out that day. He had been somewhere so terrifying in his thoughts that he needed to be grounded back in the reality of his lounge. I never left that room until I was sure that had happened.

I hope these pointers are helpful. To listen actively, to hold back from interruption, to hold back from sharing our own experiences, to stay still and alert is hard mental and physical work. But to listen is a privilege and someone who has decided to tell their story deserves our full attention—I believe we should honor them with nothing less than that.

4

Listening to Our Children

Listen earnestly to anything your children want to tell you, no matter what. If you don't listen eagerly to the little stuff when they are little, they won't tell you the big stuff when they are big, because to them all of it has always been big stuff.

As all parents know, your children do not stop being your children when they reach an age that designates them an adult. We joke that our role as parents is just to keep them alive and well until they can make their own decisions. We hope we have achieved that, knowing full well we have made mistakes along the way. Sound familiar?

We survived the terrible twos when tantrums and frustration and the learning of the words "But why?" meant that they peppered every conversation. We handed them over to an education system and hoped its philosophy married with our own. We hoped that by the end of their education, we would present to our community well-rounded young adults. People who could make their own way in the world with a passion for life, both academically and socially. We did what we as parents needed to do, to get them through their teenage years. I will say no more on this subject.

Along these roads we listened as the trials and tribulations of growing up changed from what seemed small concerns such as their best friend not playing with them to bigger concerns such as the breakup of relationships. It's that last conversation we hope our child tells us, but both of them really matter. If we have listened to the small things, truly listened, then it is much more likely that our child will tell us of the big things, primarily surrounding relationships—both friendships and romantic ones—which in my opinion are the most important parts of their lives as they get older.

I thought that my husband and I had done an OK job with our three children—we came out the end with everyone speaking to each other, which is a huge achievement for any parent. The lines of communication remain open and we are very much part of each other's lives. As adults, and two of them parents themselves now, my children tell me I was too lenient on them and I should have been tougher—they are not going to let their children get away with what they did! See what I mean? There is no right or wrong way to listen to your children, just *your* way. It remains to be seen how my children do things "better." I'm just delighted we have the sort of relationship that enables them to feel free to criticize, though it is always said with laughter and much remembering of the times they think they got away with something because I "caved."

When our firstborn son was a baby, someone gave me a parenting book called *Pajamas Don't Matter* by a Kiwi writer named Trish Gribben. It became my bible for determining what disagreements I would stand firm on and which ones I would acquiesce to. Was it worth the distress for both of us if one night, my child said he/she didn't want to wear their pajamas to bed? Did it matter? Was anyone hurt by a naked toddler sleeping soundly, thinking he/she had won a battle with their mother? The psychotherapist Philippa Perry writes about the importance of letting your child "win." That old adage about sparing the rod and spoiling the child was based on the idea that if you let them "get away" with something, they'd become terribly entitled adults. But Perry points out that a child who never feels able to exercise their will might become a submissive adult. At worst, they might fall naturally into the role of victim, find themselves open to being bullied, both as children and later as adults. It's important, she says, for children to learn to assert themselves in a situation where they feel they are "right" and you can see the logic of their argument.

Now, extrapolate that thinking out to all the thousands of requests you face as a parent. The one ingredient needed to parent in this way is to listen, fully listen, to what is being asked so your response is always a fair one, as long as it is also safe. That became my only criteria in giving in to a request I know many of my peers would say no to. I liked to think of it as a conversation between us—something we worked out together, rather than a situation in which I was the one "in charge," the judge who determined what would happen with a yes or no.

Lights out at 7 p.m., another fifteen minutes needed to finish a chapter of a loved book, no problem. No one hurt. Negotiate the fifteen minutes and don't let them extend it to thirty the next night, or the next.

Around the age of eight or nine, one of my sons decided he didn't want to sleep in the dark. We could find no bad experience, nightmare, or fear that made him frightened, he just wanted the light left on. For a few nights we left it on, only to turn it off when he was asleep. He would wake in the night, feel the need to wake us, and ask that we put the light back on. All attempts to tell him to put it on himself and get back into bed were ignored. It was our job to turn his light on at 2 a.m. Now, I'm someone who loves her sleep, so we left his light on. This continued for several months until the night he said he now wanted it turned off . . . In the end, our son sorted it out for himself.

There is one battle every parent goes through, year after year, sometimes monthly, weekly, daily. The inevitable "I don't like that" when presented with food. Once, and only once, did my husband force our firstborn to eat something he didn't want to—he got it down. Briefly. Husband wore it a short while later. I have no answer to overcoming this challenge, watching my three-year-old granddaughter ask for pasta for every meal, with the odd piece of Nutella toast. My daughter was despairing that she was not getting sufficient fruit and vegetables. Someone advised her to make smoothies instead—she now drinks her fruit and veg.

I am going out on a limb here, but this statement does come from solid, empirical research, my own experience, and that of several friends. Teenage boys are easier to listen to and to understand, and their problems and worries easier to empathize with than teenage girls. My first two children are boys, and I thought I had knocked it out of the park, getting them through the teenage years. Of course, they tell me differently now. When our daughter reached that milestone, it was a whole different ball game. I struggle to keep the smile from my face as I watch her lock horns with her three-year-old daughter, already acknowledging she is not like her easygoing, carefree brothers.

Karma.

The NHS in the UK has provided simple advice on talking to your teenager, which can be found here:

www.nhs.uk/conditions/stress-anxiety-depression/
talking-to-your-teenager/. I love their opening statement because it relates to every teenager I have met:
DO NOT JUDGE. Assume they have a good reason
for doing what they do. Show them you respect their
intelligence and are curious about the choices they've
made. And PICK YOUR BATTLES. If they only ever
hear you nagging, they will soon stop listening.

When asked if I am proud of my achievements as
an author, I always say yes—I am—but that it is overwhelming and sometimes difficult to process; that I
consider myself very lucky indeed to have met Lale
Sokolov and the direction my life has taken because
of him. In fact, what I am most proud of is the three
adult children I have raised and who I now share with
their communities, their partners and families. I am
proud of not only their achievements and the way
they parent their own children, but that they, as siblings, continue to be a strong support to each other.

When *The Tattooist of Auschwitz* was published
in Europe I went on a book tour, which took me
away from home for over a month. My daughter
was pregnant when I left. A week later, she and her
husband told me over a Skype chat that she had lost
the baby while I was in the air, flying away from my

family. She deliberately didn't tell me until she was out of hospital and at home recovering—medically, at least; the emotional recovery would take a lot longer. However, it was what she told me about the support from her two brothers during this difficult, shattering time that wrapped itself around my heart. On being admitted to hospital with a "threatened" miscarriage, on Easter Sunday, she called them. They left their families and immediately went to her. They stayed with her, allowing her husband to go home and check on their two little ones. They sacrificed being with their partners and children to be there for their sister. That my little girl immediately reached out to her brothers, knowing how they would respond, and their subsequent response, fills this mother with more pride than anything that has gone before in our lives.

Fast-forward seventeen months and I am in the delivery room with my daughter and son-in-law when their newest little man entered the world. Fast-forward again four months from that joyous moment and the importance of listening to not just what is said, but what is not said came crashing down on me. I had ignored, not seen, not interpreted the body language of this new mother, my own daughter.

Being the mother of three young children was

never going to be an easy ride, but my strong police officer daughter knew how to handle it—didn't she? Her family thought she could. Yes, she was tired, but what mother of a newborn isn't?

I went away again, this time on a seven-week book tour to support publication of my second novel, *Cilka's Journey*, when my new grandson was six weeks old. I flew away with some trepidation and a niggling fear about my daughter's health, but with hope that the brave face masking exhaustion that I'd been witnessing would pass.

Two weeks before the baby was born I had gone with my daughter and her husband when they signed a contract to buy a plot of land and build a home— their dream home. At thirty-eight weeks pregnant, she was designing the layout of their new home. A week after she gave birth, she was choosing tiles, taps, light fittings, carpets, stove, shower fittings, and on and on it went. How many downlights do you want in the kitchen, the lounge room, the bedrooms? What color brick would you like on the exterior? I cuddled a crying baby, changed his diaper, and watched as my tired, emotionally drained daughter went about creating a home for her family.

My trip over, I returned to a thriving little man and

older siblings but saw no improvement in my daughter. She was still well, still doing everything, still being the perfect parent, but something was missing. Most worryingly, I noticed a change in her behavior toward her two older children. An extremely dedicated and patient mother, she was now snapping at them for the slightest misdemeanor and ignoring their constant pleas to play with them. It also seemed to me that she was going out every day. There was always so much to do and so little time to do it in. I noticed her breastfeed her little boy and not look at him nor engage with him, with his flailing arms and hands smacking her on the breast, tugging on her clothing. I said nothing.

Christmas was fast approaching. Always the happiest time in my little girl's life—nobody loves the festive season more than she does. Rituals had been copied from her own upbringing; others created for her family. Decorations were to be hung, the tree lit up and decorated well before the designated date of December 1—she always wanted maximum time to enjoy this season. Not so this year. Yes, the tree went up, decorated over several days, not the all-at-once of the past. The children were asked what they wanted from Santa and their responses automatically bought because it required no thought on her part. Her husband was tasked with wrapping them.

She would say to us: "Can I just have one day at home with my baby, in my pajamas, to get to know him?" All too often, we said we'd make it happen, but then found a reason for her to dress, put her makeup on, and go out.

It sounds weird, but even her baby conspired against her. He never complained, rarely cried, smiled and giggled and slept while being pushed around mall after shopping mall. If only he had objected. Made it clear to his father and grandmother he wanted to stay at home, sleep in his cot fully stretched out, not folded like a pretzel into his stroller.

The signs were there. It took a photo for us to get the message, hear the cries for help we were not listening to. I went with my family to the graduation from kindergarten of my beautiful five-year-old grandson. I had the family cuddle in tight to take the happy snaps I wanted them to have to remember this day. I snapped away. I looked at the photos and there it was: on what I know would have, should have, been one of the happiest days of my girl's life, the forced smile and dead eyes looked back at me.

The next day, she refused to shower, to get out

of her track pants, to put makeup on. And the next day, and the next. Her husband didn't know what to do and called me to come around and "talk to her." He had been doing everything that needed to be done to feed, clothe, bathe, and dress their two older children. His wife had fed the baby when needed.

"I'm broken," she said, when I asked her what was wrong. "I have been screaming out for help for weeks and no one is listening," she added. "Couldn't you see? Did I have to spell it out for you?"

As her husband and I scrambled to right the wrong of not being there for her, not hearing her unspoken cries for help, my mind raced back in time—not years, just days, a few weeks. Why hadn't I been listening at one of the most important times in my daughter's life, the time when a family needs space, things done for them without being asked, given the emotional environment to bond as a larger family, with each family member finding their place in their new world?

Baby steps we are calling it as we all work together to put my broken child back together again. Already we see for every two steps forward, one back always follows. It is how we recognize this backward step and how we respond to the needs of this new mother that will determine how long it will take for her to smile again at her children, to engage with them and feel the joy once again that they bring to her life.

In my job at the hospital, I got to speak to countless parents of very sick children. It was always a source of comfort to me when they told me how their relationship, particularly their communication, changed dramatically. I wondered why so often it seemed to take a tragedy or traumatic experience for parents to listen and learn from their children. I recall one mother of a teenage daughter with a terminal illness tell me how her daughter had overheard her mother saying to her father outside her room, words to the effect of, "She's dying." Her daughter told her what she had overheard and said, "Mum, it only takes moments to die, the rest of the time we are living." This simple statement is something I will never forget. A young girl with wisdom beyond her years reminding us to live, or as Lale Sokolov would say, "If you wake up in the morning, it is a good day."

In the beautiful song "What A Wonderful World," Louis Armstrong describes how others will learn more than he could ever know. He is referring to the next generation. When my seven-year-old grandson wants to have a conversation with me about dark matter and theories of gravity, I don't look away, roll my eyes, and seek out one of his parents to "get me out of this." That he has achieved at such a young age what Armstrong sings about both delights and scares me. I explain to him that I don't know anything about dark matter and ask him to teach me what he knows. Whether his concept aligns with the experts isn't important—he wants to tell me. I want to hear, if only for the engagement with him. When his father found him ruining all their coat hangers, twisting them into designs and creations only he could visualize, and observed, "That's a lot of coat hangers," the response was, "You need a lot of coat hangers to achieve greatness."

I have discovered there is a profound difference in how I listened to my children when they were young and how I now listen to my grandchildren. I'm sure every grandparent will agree: Is it simply that we have more time and space, because we are not the stretched, stressed full-time parent? Probably. But for me there is also the realization that these young people see the world differently from me. They are subjected to a wider range of global influences than either their parents or I was at their age. I also realize that listening to them process and explain what they think they know challenges me to do the same, to think about what I know and don't know about the world. And I love it—what's not to love? These conversations with our children and grandchildren are often the most appropriate time to tell them stories of your own experience. Compare differences. Learn from each other.

When my children were young, more often than I care to admit, I found myself using the words, "When I was your age . . ." My childhood experiences were so utterly different from theirs—different country, for starters. Different times. I was born at the end of an era, in a rural setting, where children were seen and not heard, where discipline was valued above all, and in which the concept of a child having "feelings" didn't really exist—certainly, we were not, as I've outlined earlier, listened to. My children were aware of this and were fascinated by how differently I had chosen to parent them, but that didn't stop at least one, and sometimes all three, miming playing a violin and humming the tune to the television series *The Twilight Zone*. They still do it to me now. I didn't listen then, and it still doesn't stop me from dispensing words of wisdom now they are adults. They expected me to listen to them; I honored that, and in return I feel I have a right to be heard. And I believe that I have something to offer—as we all do. I have lived a life and have experience of so many things, so many instances where I feel I did things the right way—or the wrong way. What I believe is that my children and I have been in dialogue since the day they were born and I hope that we will continue this way for many years to come. The dynamics shift as the years pass, but the conversation continues to flow.

When they were children, these conversations happened frequently over dinner. It was important to us that each evening, we sat down together for dinner, no matter how busy everyone was, what kind of a day my husband and I had had: it was a coming together as a family unit. With three children, a ten-year age gap between them, and a typically dominant middle child, I looked for ways to make this an enjoyable experience for everyone. I swapped our rectangular dining table for a round one so that there was no fighting over who sat at the head. I wanted the conversation about each other's day to be equal—no talking over each other, no one person dominating. By accident, a supermarket green pepper mill became known as the "talkie thing." When someone placed it in front of their plate, we all listened to what they had to say. Eventually it would be picked up by another sibling as they claimed their right to speak and we all listened. As parents, we subtly controlled the length of conversation by taking the talkie thing, asking another child about their day, and placing it in front of them. No one ever abused the talkie thing, everyone was to be listened to and respected for what they wanted to say.

And that brings me to the word *respect*. How can we expect our children to respect us and what we say if we don't respect their opinions, their concerns and demonstrate this by listening to what they have to say? I didn't and don't always get it right, but I try. Also, perhaps particularly when they were teenagers, I didn't always agree with what they were saying. But I listened and made sure that they knew that I was doing so—those active listening skills apply at whatever age your child is. That is not to say everything your toddler says to you is worthy of an in-depth conversation—in many instances a small acknowledgment is all that is required. They will often move on from what they have been telling you faster than you can comprehend what it was they were saying. Often, they grow frustrated by their failure to get you to understand them—at which point their grasp of language fails them—and this can be tricky. Equally, as frustrating as it can be when you feel the time is right to tell them something deep and meaningful—at any age—you must remember they themselves may not have learned the importance of listening. Think back to my grandson's frustration at his sister refusing to listen to him.

Often children have wisdom beyond their years. They are this way because of the experiences and circumstances in their lives and because they are little humans, with all of the intelligence that we have—I suspect people sometimes forget this. In any situation I found challenging with my children, I used to try to remember what I'd been like at their particular age and how I'd felt about my parents' reaction to something. Teenage high jinks? We've all done it. Lying to our parents—where's the adult who never did that as a young person? In fact, show me someone who doesn't tell the odd white lie, the odd sin of omission. We all do it. A desperate desire for privacy, for independence, for freedom? Same again. Walk in your children's shoes and you'll find it easier to see it their way and to work out how to respond.

It's also essential to remember that we can't shield our children from all negative, traumatic events—we can't protect them from everything, no matter how much we'd like to—and that these events will also shape their thinking, their vision of the world, their personalities.

Often at the funerals for stillborn babies I attended in the course of my work at the hospital, siblings would be brought along with the parents. On many occasions I witnessed the parents supporting each other as a young child looked on. Lost, forlorn, overwhelmed by the chapel with its sad row of small white coffins, and by dozens of strangers also struck down by grief. One of the social workers in attendance would always be on hand to swoop down on a distressed child to provide comfort, supporting parents to envelop that child into their circle. On many occasions, with the permission of the parents, the social worker would take the sibling back into the chapel after the service and explain why they were there, on this, the first Wednesday of the month. The child might be invited to light a candle for the brother or sister they never got to meet. Training, compassion, simply being decent human beings enabled these wonderful professionals to make a difference.

I know we are told to talk to children in an "age-appropriate" manner, but we must be alert to the children whose age does not marry up with their life lived. Only by listening to them, truly listening to them, can we help them process their thoughts, identify concerns that may arise if their feelings are not validated and acknowledged.

I was lucky to have a great-grandfather and a father who listened to me and whom I loved to listen to. Sadly, my mother, as I have said, very seldom made herself available to me to talk to, nor felt the need to talk to me in any meaningful way. This situation did not change when I became an adult, and a mother myself. I resolved to be the opposite with my own daughter—and to take every opportunity I could to engage with young people.

Growing up, my brothers and I took the lead from our parents. However, as adults, we talk and share our lives constantly. Other than my immediate family, it will always be one of my brothers I now turn to when I need someone to listen to me. They in turn reach out to me. When I look in the mirror, I realize it is my turn to be the older, sometimes wiser, person in the lives of not only the young people in my life, but any young person with whom I am privileged to speak.

The Tattooist of Auschwitz has been published in a

Young Adult edition, something of which I am extremely proud. Visiting schools and speaking to teenagers is for me pure joy. To be in a room with one hundred or so fourteen-year-olds who pay me the respect of listening to me intently is truly humbling. I know they have been listening because of the amazing questions they ask. As they gather around me at the end of my talk, instead of going to their next class, I send up a quiet "thank you" to Lale Sokolov for having told me his story, so that I can pass it on to a new generation.

It is not only older people whose stories have had a profound impact on my life. Many years ago, I came into contact with a teenage boy in the hospital with a terminal illness. To pass the time during treatment, he played games on a handheld gaming device. I was told he had mastered all the levels of the games he had. A quick phone call to the company who designed and sold the games resulted in an offer of two new unreleased games. A young man, a designer from the company, turned up in the social work department to deliver them. We got chatting and he told me he wanted an excuse to leave the office, so had decided to hand-deliver the games rather than mail them. Instead of taking them from him, I arranged for the social worker looking after the teenager to take the visitor to the ward so he could hand them to the patient personally.

What transpired from this meeting between a terminally ill patient and a game designer was a friendship of profound beauty. Several times the designer turned up in my office on his way to the ward to thank me for putting him in touch with this boy. He told me about his privileged life, that he had never known children could get so sick they might die. He met the boy's family and other teenagers in the ward. His life had been changed, he told me, by having his eyes opened to the tragedy of young people spending long periods in the hospital, undergoing painful treatment. He was overwhelmed by their positive attitudes to their illnesses and the hope they and their families clung to for remission, for recovery. He himself had opened up to the patients, shared information about himself, showed his own vulnerability. He had become a regular visitor, so at ease with the patients that they played practical jokes on him. He remained connected to the teenager, to the end, and their friendship was a great comfort to them both.

Practical Tips for Listening to Children

Here are some thoughts around listening to children that might be useful. They apply not only to *our* children, of course, but to any young person we might encounter. The essential thing is to be an active listener: pay attention, respect the child talking to you, respect what is being said, no matter how trivial or unimportant it seems to you. I can only repeat: if you don't listen to the small stuff, you may not be told the big stuff.

Time—that's the secret to listening to a child. And taking the time to listen to a child when they are little is the key to a close and secure relationship, which pays dividends during the more challenging years of adolescence. I understand that it's not always possible to drop what you are doing in the midst of a busy life, but if you want your child to know how important they are to you, if you want to give them confidence and self-esteem, you need to find the time to listen to them.

When my three kids were small, I was a busy working mother. In between work, school pickup, cooking tea, supervising homework, and throwing the clothes in the wash there wasn't a lot of time for those one-to-one moments. I knew that, the kids knew that—we managed. But if I sensed one of them had something on their mind, and there was no immediate opportunity to sit down to listen, I used to find the best thing was to ask them to help me with a routine task. It's surprising what a child will tell you when you are folding laundry together, or watering the garden, or setting the table.

Teachers often single out a child they are concerned about and ask them for special help—preparing a display of work, for instance, or sorting out the books in a classroom. Not only does this make the child feel important, it's an opportunity to allow them to speak without addressing their concerns directly. You can do something like this at home. The key thing is to keep the focus on the job at hand, however trivial, to create a neutral safe space—and not to make direct eye contact. If the child falters or lapses into silence, you can always return to the work you are doing to give them time to gather their thoughts and confidence: "Now, how many more pins do I need here?," "We've finished the towels, shall we pair the socks?"

I realize that domestic chores don't cut much ice with most teenagers, so how do you manage then? If you've fostered a relationship of trust with your child from an early age, you should have a firm basis on which to negotiate the trickier years of adolescence. However, as teenagers widen their social circles and begin to rely on their peers rather than their parents for emotional support and validation, it can be challenging to keep the conversation going. However hard it is, and however many unrewarding grunts you get in response to a simple question like "how was school today?"—keep going! The work you put in now will pay dividends in the relationship you build with them as adults.

Try to create a situation in which your children speak, and you are "present" to listen. For us, it was the table and the talkie thing that worked for the whole family, but there are other ways of getting a child or teenager alone in a situation in which they might speak. The car is good—you are together, but you are both looking straight ahead. For six years I drove my daughter to her high school every morning. We had to drive past the police academy and would see the recruits training outside. Often, we commented on the force as a profession. My daughter joked that she liked seeing them running around the track or out on the street, that being an athlete, she could do that part of the job. Six years after leaving school, working, and traveling, she was sworn in as a police officer.

Top Tips for Listening to Your Children:

- Find an activity you can share together.
- Avoid direct eye contact.
- Ask open-ended questions.
- If the conversation stalls, return to the job at hand to allow the child time to gather themselves and then go back to an earlier point in the story and ask a factual question to show that you've listened.
- Pay attention to the way you hold yourself physically. Avoid folding your arms and keep your body movements slow and deliberate.
- If your child wants to tell you something and you just aren't able to listen then and there, plan a moment when you can—and make sure they know they will have your

undivided attention then. You might say, "I really want to hear about that—how about you and I make tea together later?"

- Avoid a prescriptive response. If your child wants to tell you about a specific problem, ask them what they think the best solution might be. If they persist in asking for advice, offer a few suggestions and ask them to choose. Praise the choice they make.

- Don't forget to ask them about how they are *feeling* about what they have told you. When they have finished, make sure they have said everything they needed to say.

- Not everything has to be serious. You can use gentle humor in your responses, but not sarcasm—it's never helpful.

- Never dismiss what your child is telling you. Their worries may seem unimportant or ridiculous to you, but they are important to them—and they have chosen to share them with you. Honor their trust.

- As psychotherapist Philippa Perry says, all behavior is a form of communication, right down to toddler tantrums. So try to listen and respond to that behavior. What has triggered it and what might they be trying to tell you?

- A child doesn't always pick the "right" moment to tell you something. Do your best to acknowledge what they are saying, no matter what the circumstances. Do your best to listen, or if that's not possible, then ask if they can tell you later. But you might find that when you try to re-create "the moment" it has passed.

- Pick your battles—this is the "pajamas don't matter" rule and it applies whether you are dealing with a toddler insisting on wearing their rain boots to school on a hot summer's day or a teenager pushing the boundaries of what you will allow them to do. The key question is always safety, isn't it? And does it really matter?

- Be open and prepared for what you might hear—it mightn't be what you'd hoped, wanted—it might involve an admission that you are surprised or even upset by.

- Equally, be prepared to be surprised by a completely different interpretation of a particular event or situation—you might find that you are criticized, or accused of behavior in a way that feels unfair or unreasonable, but it's very important to listen. Above all, try not to react with anger.

- DO NOT JUDGE. Or keep those judgments to yourself, at least until you've had time to temper your response.
- With younger children, try to make the conversations inspiring. I might try to follow up my grandson's explanation of gravity with a story about the simplicity of my childhood, or his father's as a way of encouraging him to think about how much the world has changed.
- Listen carefully to what a child might be trying to tell you behind a particular story or anecdote.
- Remember to practice those active listening skills—they apply to any situation in which you are the listener, regardless of the age of the child.

5

Listening to Ourselves

The world is giving you answers each day. Learn to listen.

Listening to ourselves. Easier said than done, isn't it? What do I mean by this? Later, I'll discuss the cost of listening, and the importance of making sure that we listen to our own responses, that we practice self-care, that we do not make what we hear into our own problems or trauma. Here, I am talking about trusting our instincts when we are listening, and learning to trust ourselves.

A key element of being a good listener, being a

support to others, is having a good and solid relationship with yourself. You need to treat yourself like a good and reliable friend, otherwise how can you offer that same friendship to others? Essential to this is remembering always to be kind to yourself—if you're not, then who will be? The point is that we can't help others, understand others, if we don't do this for ourselves. We all have those moments of self-doubt, self-blame, shame: "I shouldn't have said that," "I should have listened properly to what someone was trying to tell me," "I sounded silly when I suggested that." And in those moments, it's important to do what you would with a friend—tell yourself to forget it, move on, you were doing your best. I think this last point is worthy of repeating: you can only do the best you can at any given point on any given day. Guilt and self-blame are only ever negative thoughts.

During my years working in the social work department at the hospital, I connected daily to patients, their families, their friends. They presented often during tragic and traumatic times in their lives, and as office manager, I was often the first person they saw. I am not trained as a social worker, but my boss called me "the occasional counselor." I am in awe of the social work profession. I witnessed so many times the difference social workers can make in supporting a person through the worst times of their lives. The death of a much-loved partner, of a parent, a sibling, a dear friend. However, it was the loss of newborns, which sadly I saw many times, that I carry in my heart and in my head. And will do for the remainder of my days.

I write about this aspect of my life because there was barely a week of my twenty years' work in the hospital that I was not involved in the death of a baby, be it through miscarriage, stillbirth, or neonatal death. I began this chapter reflecting on how we should listen to ourselves and protect ourselves from others' grief. There were many times when I did not do this for myself and I am eternally grateful to the hospital staff who helped me manage my own feelings, particularly my boss, who took great care to remind me of my role in these families' lives—to listen, empathize, and make a difference, no matter how small.

What I remember most about my time involved in the perinatal loss program was the little things that at the time seemed inconsequential but had a profound impact. As I have mentioned earlier, once a month, the hospital held a funeral/memorial service for the babies lost in the past four weeks. I assisted with the administration, in conjunction, with the chaplains, funeral directors and the cemetery. On most first Wednesdays of the month, I attended the service. Twelve times a year over twenty years adds up to a lot of first Wednesdays of the month!

Knowing what those of us involved had to manage on these Wednesdays at 10 a.m. never got easier. A new month. New families. Sometimes families we'd met before who were saying farewell to a second baby. Sometimes, I had already met the parents; sometimes I hadn't. Often, I would meet them when they brought to the department clothing, tokens of love, mementos, photographs they wanted placed in the coffin with their baby. I would receive them, assuring the parents of the care we would take in placing these special objects with their baby, that their baby would be dressed in these precious garments. On many occasions I did this personally. Talking to the baby as I dressed him or her, I would tell them who the people in the photo were; that they were being given a drawing their three-year-old sister/brother had made for them; that this was a flower their mother had picked from her garden that morning; I would read them the letter their grandmother wrote, telling them who their family were, where they were from, and how they would be loved and remembered.

Out of all the mementos and gifts I placed in a coffin, one stands out for me and flooded back to me recently when my five-year-old grandson showed me his first marbles and asked me to play with him. A grieving mother and father stood in front of me and I listened as the mother handed me several items, explaining what they were and why she wanted them placed with her baby. The little jacket she had knitted was way too big for her prematurely born baby, but it was the first thing she had made for her expected firstborn and she wanted him to have it. Her partner stood beside her, his head down, pain at hearing his partner, between sobs, explain the significance of each item, etched on his face. He had one of his hands in his pocket and I could hear something clicking. As his wife dissolved into tears, he hugged her and then looking over her shoulder, he removed his hand from his pocket and looked at me: in his hand were two marbles.

"These are the first two marbles my father gave me. I had many as a boy, lost some, won others, but I never risked losing these. I wanted to teach my son how to play marbles. Would you please take one, choose one, your choice, and give it to my son? I'll keep the other." As I reached out to take one, he closed his fist and his eyes briefly before opening them and letting me take one of the marbles. I chose the blue one, leaving him with the yellow—I don't know why.

Two years later, that father reappeared in my office, his yellow marble in one hand, cell phone in the other, the biggest smile on his face. He came to show me the photos of his newborn daughter, hours old. He had brought the marble into the hospital with him when his wife went into labor. He told me I had chosen the right marble—he felt the yellow one was more suited to his new baby girl.

How does this story connect to this chapter? The first time I met this father, and during my interaction with him, including taking the marble from his hand, I remained silent. There were no words I could say that would help this man. He had all he needed right then and there, with his partner in his arms. They walked away from me without a backward glance. As they should. I had listened to myself: there was nothing I could do or say right then that was going to make a scrap of difference to the pain this couple was living through. I did what they asked me to do: choose the marble. On the second occasion we met, I listened again, but this time I gave him a hug. It felt like the right thing to do. Again, there weren't really words to express what he had told me. My instincts told me that physical contact was not only appropriate for him, but also for me—he had reached out and taken the trouble to come and tell me this wonderful piece of news and so I reached out in response. This type of physical contact between staff and a patient's family member was not encouraged, or probably considered professional, but there are times when it seemed to be the right thing, the human thing to do. I'd like to think—no, I believe—in this instance it was right.

My postscript to this story—I gave my grandson the longest hug (thankfully, he loves grandma hugs), then tried to teach him the tricks I had learned playing marbles as a girl.

Following your instinct—your gut, as we sometimes say—when listening to others and knowing when and how to respond is not always easy. The right thing won't always be obvious. There are times when you know your interaction with someone is going to be a "one-off"—a shop assistant, the person standing in front of you in a line to board a plane or enter a theater, places where a brief conversation is merited. You have something in common here, traveling somewhere, enjoying the same show, buying something the shop assistant is invested in selling you. A casual conversation should be just that, casual. The only thing I'd say here is to judge the moment and respond to the cues of others. Equally, while we must always be polite and gentle, and treat others as we'd hope to be treated, we don't have to engage with everyone constantly—that way lies madness and a lot of time wasted.

Here is a story about a casual encounter that took on huge significance. I don't go to the theater as much as I would like. However, the opportunity to see the delightfully funny Billy Connolly a few years ago was not to be missed. As I lined up with my husband to take our seats, the woman in front asked me if I had seen Billy before. I proudly told her I had seen him in concert in Christchurch several years earlier. She told me this was the first time she would see him live, that she and her husband had enjoyed his sense of humor for decades. I noted she didn't seem to be with another person but said nothing. However, it didn't stop her talking. She told me they had bought tickets for the two of them many months earlier, but her husband had died a few weeks ago. She thought about not coming on her own but decided her husband would want her to and she was honoring him by being there. On impulse, trusting my instinct, I asked if she would like to meet up after the concert for a drink and to share our reviews. We met and had a nightcap, talking over each other as we agreed Billy Connolly is the funniest man going. We did not talk about her recently deceased husband, nor did we talk about meeting again. And we didn't. But every time Mr. Connolly graces my television screen, or I see his beautiful face in a magazine, I think about her. I like to think that my husband and I made just a tiny bit of difference that day and she certainly made that evening even more special for us.

Timing. Time and place, the little things we do not look for, the people we connect with accidentally, can often impact us more than a lifelong friendship or relationship. You don't have to "put yourself out there," just be in the time and place you are in and the universe has a way of coming to you. Or at least, be open, be patient, don't be afraid—this is my approach to human interaction. And so often you will benefit hugely from these chance encounters. This doesn't happen daily, weekly, or monthly. That is the beauty of living—you never know. All you can do is be intuitive about the people who pass through your life, use your gut instinct to engage or not engage. As I've said above—feel free not to engage! Listen to yourself, talk to yourself if you want—nothing wrong with that, I'm doing it while writing this. I have learned to make myself smile, not to be dependent on others, though I love it when others have that effect on me.

Those years working in a hospital could be tough. My times with Lale, hearing his stories and the research I carried out when we weren't together, sometimes brought me down. Being a writer, becoming a public figure, has been an overwhelming joy but it also comes with its own pressures, and being a public figure can mean people feel able to criticize. They are entitled to their opinions, but my response to this is a human one. My husband always knew when I asked him to find the DVD of the movie *Airplane* that I needed a good long laugh. It is my go-to. If it's a good cry, then the Bette Midler movie *Beaches* does the job. To become emotionally overwhelmed, really get lost in something, it's *Out of Africa*, as much for the beautiful music as the story line of love, hope, and courage. I use movies to nourish the emotion I need to feel—I suppose you could call it a form of catharsis. I know what I'm feeling but somehow channeling it through the prism of one of these much-loved, often-watched films allows me to experience those emotions in a "safe" environment and distance myself from whatever has left me feeling distressed.

When I was adapting *The Tattooist of Auschwitz* into a novel from my own screenplay, locked away in my sister-in-law and brother's cabin on Big Bear Mountain in California in the middle of winter, I used music to put my head and heart into the space I needed. When I sat down for the first time each day to write, I spent the first nine minutes listening to Henryk Górecki's Symphony no. 3, op. 36 "Symphony of Sorrowful Songs," recorded by Kasprzyk and the Szymanowski State Philharmonic Orchestra, with vocals by Zofia Kilanowicz. Listening to this beautiful, haunting music, I also listened to the sound of my own heart beating—I was connecting my body and my mind. The faces of my family played on rewind in my head, my love for them so intense I felt it physically. I remembered Lale Sokolov, this man I was honoring, who sadly had not lived long enough to see his story in print. As the music ended and I opened my eyes, inevitably I would wipe away tears. And then I would write. For hours. When it was time to "save" and "shut down" for the day, it was again music that now ended my day. The passion with which Andra Day sings her powerful song "Rise Up" would lift me from my chair, put a huge smile on my face as I fist-pumped and told Lale we were on our way to sharing his story with the world.

I rejoiced in my decision to say yes to meeting a man whose wife had just died and who wanted to tell his story to someone. It was the busiest time of the year, three weeks before Christmas, but I listened to my gut saying, *GO, what have you got to lose?* I am grateful that on the whole, every time my instinct has told me to do something, take a risk, it has been the right decision.

Occasionally we can get it wrong, and sometimes I have to force myself to ignore that nagging little inner voice saying, *give it a go.* But I have learned to trust my instincts. When I fled my birth family and the claustrophobic belt that tied me to a small town, I didn't just flee to the next town or city, but to a different country, arriving in Australia on my own, aged nineteen. I have no regrets for what was an impulsive decision—my husband, three children, and five grandchildren are testament to this being the best impulse I ever acted on.

I suppose I have at times in my life been guilty of thinking that moving away, or more correctly, *running* away, from personal problems that I don't want to face is the best answer. It is an answer, but it's not really the best one. Thankfully, I had the love and support of my family to guide me, to help me refocus on who I was, on who we could be as a family. They also helped me understand what I wanted to run away from.

When my oldest brother died in mid-2018 in New Zealand, I returned and reconnected with friends there, finding a spiritual connection to my homeland that I feel nowhere else in the world. On my return to Australia, I thought I wanted to move back to the country of my birth, to wrap myself in the uniqueness of the people and the land. Of course, it was grief pulling me back there. My family in Australia listened to me, understood my desire to "go home," then reminded me that if I moved away, I would be leaving my children and grandchildren—I would be leaving the living to be with the dead. It was enough that they would have supported me, had I been successful in persuading my husband to uproot. They reminded me of the connection that binds me to my family and friends and to all that lies ahead.

I love the word "connection"—research professor of social work Dr. Brené Brown says we can't have connection without allowing ourselves to be vulnerable with others, letting others "see" who we are, and taking the risk that they might not like what they see. We can have a connection with another person at the smallest level, exchanging a glance with someone choosing the same brand of cereal after considering the many displayed before us. Then there are the major connections that bring two people together through a shared interest that reveals many other shared interests—a link back to a third party and with time and conversation, a string of connections form as you share stories.

Not long ago, I was traveling on the subway in New York on a cold, wet, wintry day, there to launch my novel *Cilka's Journey*. Along with others, I needed to get from Lower Manhattan to Upper Manhattan. Ordinarily, we would have taken a cab but the locals I was traveling with, new to my life, assured me we would reach our destination far quicker taking the subway.

On a crowded, peak-hour train one of my companions shared with me her pride in her teenage son, who has a specific learning disability. I do not know why she chose this public place to confide in me, or why she shared information about her son, but she did, and I was humbled to hear it. Someone very close to me back in Australia, with whom this person has a working relationship, also had a son a few years older, with the same disability. Both of these people are still in my life and now they are connected independently of me. I'm so glad that I could make this connection between two people I value so highly. I know they correspond on matters other than their professional connection. What transpires between them rightly stays that way. As important as it is to put yourself into someone else's life, knowing when not to, or to withdraw, is equally important.

Since *The Tattooist of Auschwitz* was released, in January 2018, I have received thousands of emails from many countries. Most of them are short, simply expressing thanks and gratitude for telling this story. However, many of them go on to tell me about a tragic or traumatic event in their life, often quite recent, where hope for a future was taken from them. In reading Lale and Gita's story, they have found hope. Reading of their love, courage, and survival in one of the darkest times in recent history, they tell me, has enabled them to take the first steps to finding their lost dreams for themselves and loved ones. Then there are the many emails from readers who have their own amazing story and ask for advice and assistance in finding a way to tell it. I also hear from readers who have connected with me personally at a talk I have given, or watched me in an interview on television, or listened to me on the radio. I feel so humbled that so many people have been touched by the stories I have told and want to reach out to me.

However, the email I received in South Africa, which led me to visit Israel twice in six months, stands out to me over and above all the others I have received. Because of it, I have told another amazing story of courage, survival, and hope. This time I wrote of the love of three sisters. What I heard in the voice of a ninety-two-year-old woman drew me to her, to her country, to her story. Sometimes it doesn't take much—gut and instincts honed from decades of being open to listening tell you what to do. Making yourself vulnerable in meeting strangers, knowing you will need to be honest and open about yourself before they can be open with you, will bring rewards.

On other occasions, I have replied to correspondence and visited those writing to me because it was the right thing to do. It is about acknowledging the effort made by those who write in the first instance and validating their vulnerability in sharing their feelings on reading about Lale, Gita, and Cilka.

On that same trip to New York, I arranged to visit a drug rehabilitation center in New Jersey after I received a letter from a counselor there. She told me that several of the young people at the center, who were recovering and rehabilitating from drug abuse, had been affected by Lale Sokolov's story, finding inspiration and hope in his survival.

For over two hours I sat and talked to around fifty young men and women, telling them untold stories of Lale and Gita, and hearing their own stories of survival. As tragic as their pasts had been, I was so inspired by their determination to deal with their drug problems and to find paths forward to give them the lives they now dared to dream of. Studying, working, striving to build meaningful relationships and give back to their communities were goals I hope they will achieve. I was told how many of them would not be able to return to their families who lived nearby because a family member was still "using." They accepted this was the way it had to be if they were going to live, like Lale and Gita, the best life they could. The professionals who worked, taught, and supported these individuals and their choices were a further inspiration to me. They were devoted to their center and worked tirelessly with little funding to encourage and support the bravery of these young people who were standing up for themselves. I thank them most sincerely for contacting me and welcoming me to their center. On my return to Australia I received a lovely folder of letters from each person I met that day, expressing what our time together had meant to them.

I want them to know how much meeting them meant to me. I proudly tell of my time with them, I think of them often, I feel blessed to have been invited into their circle. I listened to them, they listened to me, I listened to my inner voice telling me this would be an experience I would treasure—so I did it.

Here is a story my brother Ian told me, about learning to listen to himself:

Ian's Story

The day after I turned sixteen, my mother told me I wasn't going to school the next day—I would be going up to Auckland. I could count on one hand the number of times I had been to Auckland and I thought the trip was a birthday present.

On the train there, I was told we were visiting the recruiting officer of the New Zealand Navy. My older brother had joined up four years earlier and I thought we would be visiting him; I didn't initially register the significance of the words "recruitment officer."

Taken into an office, I remained silent as my mother conducted the interview on my behalf. The next thing I knew, I was being asked to sign a document. I was agreeing to serve in the Navy for twelve years. I was to commence training immediately, but the twelve-year term would not start running for two more years, when I turned eighteen, as I was still a minor. It never occurred to me to argue with my mother; I unquestioningly believed she knew what was best for me. How wrong could I be?

Within a few weeks I was decked out in a Navy uniform and training alongside dozens of other young, naive, impressionable men. There were no women in our group. From day one, I hated Navy life. For two and a half years I endured the humiliation, hazing, and abuse that went with training. The only saving grace for me was the friendships I made.

Three months shy of my nineteenth birthday, I went for a motorbike ride with two fellow sailors. On a country road outside of Auckland a car plowed into us—my two friends died, I didn't. After their funerals, I decided I did not want to continue another day in Her Majesty's Royal New Zealand Navy. I put in the paperwork for discharge from my contract, as I was now an adult. My captain, a noncommissioned officer, asked to see me after he received my request and told me in no uncertain terms that I would not be discharged—I was to serve my time, the Navy was going to make a man out of me.

The rules allowed me to apply for discharge each month. I did so each month, and each time I was refused. The day after my third rejection I was walking through the naval yard with friends when we were stopped by our captain. He eyeballed me, got into my personal space, and told me he didn't like my hair and I was to get it cut. I knew he was trying to humiliate me, but by then I no longer cared—I just wanted out. The next day, I went into a hair salon in Auckland and got my hair cut.

On Monday, he sought me out and inspected my hair.

"I told you to get your hair cut."

"I did, sir."

He said it was clearly not a Navy cut, where had I been? I told him the name of the place in Auckland. He asked me how much I had paid, and I told him $15.00, standard for a haircut in those days. He attempted to ridicule me in front of my friends, telling me I had wasted my money. He ordered me to get in his vehicle as he was taking me to the Navy hairdresser, but I refused and walked away from him.

I was subsequently taken to his superior officer, and his superior officer until I found myself in front of the commanding officer of the base. When he told me I was to have my hair cut, I said no. I had followed instructions and already done so.

I was immediately charged with "willful disobedience of a direct order" and placed in a cell. For the record, if two people disobey a direct order, it is considered mutiny. It was a Friday, the next day was my nineteenth birthday, and my parents had planned a party for all my Navy mates at their home, an hour south of Auckland.

I celebrated my nineteenth birthday sitting in a cell, while my mates went to my parents' home and had "my" party.

The court martial took place on the Monday. My representative told me I was to say nothing, that he would ask for lenience as I was grieving at having seen my two closest friends die. The CO was present and told the presiding judge what had transpired. The judge asked me if I had willfully disobeyed a direct order from my commanding officer. I did not keep quiet as my lawyer had asked.

"No, sir, I told him to fuck off and I'm telling you to do the same!"

Needless to say, I was found guilty and sentenced to nine months in the military prison.

Back to the cells for me. A couple of days went by and I had to undergo a physical examination to ensure I could withstand imprisonment—I passed.

The day I was to be transferred to the prison I was picked up by the signals officer for the base. He asked me if we could stop off at the signals office, as he wanted to pick up the incoming mail. I was in no hurry to be locked away.

He returned a short while later and sat in the cab of the truck.

"Tell me your name and date of birth."

I told him.

"This is your lucky day," he told me.

He then read one of the signals he had picked up. The commodore of Auckland had to sign off on all sailors being sent to serve a prison sentence. He noted that I had made several requests for a discharge, I clearly did not want to be in the Navy, and I was to be discharged immediately as "services no longer required." This discharge was only one step above a dishonorable discharge.

I spent a couple of days in prison while the necessary paperwork was completed and then was taken to the bus stop and sent home.

After my mother got over the shock of my no longer being in the Navy, she said, "Well, I'll get in touch with Mr. X, (our local friendly police officer) and ask him to get you into the police force."

I didn't unpack.

I have subsequently carved out the life I wanted, the life that was right for me, and what a life I have had! I have lived in several countries, had a successful business career, and a wonderful family too.

Practical Tips for Listening to Yourself

How do you go about making the important decisions in your life? Some people earnestly compile lists of pros and cons; others look to friends or family for advice. Many of us rely on "gut instinct"—but where does that instinct come from and what shapes it? And how do we learn to trust it and listen to ourselves?

We are all of us the products of our life experience. A happy, secure child will become a resilient adult, with the resources and confidence to cope with whatever life throws at them. Someone less secure is more likely to struggle, to be less certain that their choices are going to be good ones, to feel that they can survive life's curveballs. They may indeed end up making poor choices. But all of us, however we were raised and whatever good or bad decisions we've taken in the past, can learn to listen to ourselves. It's taken me many years to learn to trust my own instincts, but I do now—and this is how I do it.

First of all, you have to learn to trust yourself. Many of us, myself included, spend our years as young people fulfilling others' ideas of who we are and how we should behave. Call it conformity, call it duty, call it a wish to please, but most of us put our own instincts to one side and do what is expected of us—and plenty of us carry on like this for the whole of our lives. It doesn't have to be like this, but years of schooling and societal pressures can conspire to eradicate what makes us distinct individuals.

I'm asking you to leave all that aside and go back to your earliest memories as a child. As children, if we are able to explore our own interests, we discover instinctively where they lie; from adolescence, these preferences tend to be overlaid with the expectations of others. Think back to your childhood and ask yourself:

- What did I choose to do when I had time to myself?
- Did I like playing alone, or did I prefer the company of others?
- What toy or toys did I play with the most?
- (If you chose to read) What were the books I was most drawn to? Puzzle books? True stories? Fantasy and fairy tales?

- What was I most proud of achieving as a child?
- What imaginary games did I play?
- What activity made me feel at my happiest and most sure of myself?

You may be surprised by some of the answers—and you might find that they sit a long way from where your life is right now. But by asking yourself these questions, you are connecting with yourself and your instincts at the most fundamental level, unfettered by the overlay of experience. You are beginning to listen to your true self.

As a child, I was always drawn to stories of the past. I wanted to know *why* things happened, *how* people responded, *what it was like* to experience what they had been through. I suppose that what I was driven by was incredible curiosity—and it is that curiosity that I see now as a pattern running through my life. I didn't always pay attention to it, but when I look back, there is a thread connecting listening to Gramps to listening to Lale Sokolov. Now I understand this, it has made listening to *myself* much easier.

Top Tips for Listening to Yourself

- **Write stuff down.** As I've described earlier, when I was spending time with Lale, I created a spreadsheet that recorded how our visit had been, how he'd seemed. Crucially, I also kept a note of how I felt on that day, because instinct told me that this was just as important.

- **Trust your gut**, but equally learn to distinguish between instinct and impulse—something I've spent years working on. Count to ten in order to "hear" whether you are doing the right thing. Leave that email in your drafts overnight; write a list of pros and cons before making a big life decision. Those who know me well will point out this is not a tip I practice as much as I should!

- **Find a way to "go to your happy place"** when you hear something distressing. I used to reach down and pat the heads of Lale's dogs Tootsie and Bam Bam whenever I felt distressed or overwhelmed by what he was telling me. When I'm away, I often get out my phone and flick through pictures of my beloved family. Music also has the power to transport me to another time and place.

- **Accept that what you feel** in relation to a person, a situation, and what you are hearing won't always be the same. We change, we grow, we are in ourselves sometimes more robust and patient than at other times. Sometimes there's no obvious reason why this may be.

- **Not feeling able to cope, not connecting with someone**, isn't always your fault. It might be theirs; it is probably no one's fault.

- **Remind yourself always** what you have to be grateful for—perhaps also note this down. This can be as simple as being a parent, being able to see the sunrise, or in my case, sunset— I'm not a morning person!

Now, whenever I'm faced with a choice or an opportunity and I don't know what to do, I frame my decision by thinking back to that child and to the unfettered choices I made then. Of course, there are practical matters and the care and responsibility for others to take into consideration, so unfettered choices are much harder for us to make as adults, but I still believe that listening to ourselves is key to making good decisions. And if there's an opportunity to listen to someone with a story, I'm going to take it!

6

Helping to Find a Narrative of Hope, or Honoring the Narrative

"My mother/father/grandmother/grandfather won't talk to me, won't tell me about their time during the Holocaust. How can I make them?"

Countless times this statement has been said to me. Countless. My response is simple: you can't. I asked a friend of mine, a leading psychiatrist in Melbourne, whether I was doing harm to Lale in letting him talk to me at such an emotional level, given he was also grieving the loss of Gita. I was talking to him not as a professional but as a friend, in a social setting. This man already knew a great deal about my relationship with Lale. He assured me I wasn't, that Lale would never tell me something he didn't want to talk about. This was so reassuring to hear. And, as I have already written, I know Lale took a lot of his story to his grave. My psychiatrist friend told me he was more concerned about me looking after myself than he was about Lale. He could see I was invested in our friendship and was at pains to point out that I needed to take care of myself.

"Do what you know is the right thing for the both of you," he told me. "You can't go wrong if you follow your instincts, protect yourself first and by default, you will protect Lale."

How right he was.

Knowing this, or because of this, I took my responsibility very seriously. I knew I must be sure to tell Lale's story true to his memory—I have included nothing he didn't tell me. Although I made sure that I verified everything he told me, because I was aware of the extreme sensitivities around this subject. I only included details that I could verify from another source. But when his stories didn't always match up with researched facts, I also knew I was not telling THE story of the Holocaust, I was telling A Holocaust story—Lale's story.

My initial thoughts were to write a memoir; I even went to a Memoir Writing Workshop—for a day—it was a five-day workshop. I knew after one day the style and rules of a memoir did not suit the way Lale wanted his story told. I saw Lale's story played out on a screen. Big or small, it didn't matter. Having attended many screenwriting classes, seminars, and workshops, and being familiar with the disciplines of writing a screenplay, I decided that was the way I would work. It was only after several years trying to have the script developed, that I made the decision to adapt the screenplay into a novel. I am not a historian, and so many brilliant minds have written and recorded the story of the Holocaust, and so I chose to use the medium of fiction to re-create all that Lale told me in our three years of friendship.

Lale only chose to talk to me because Gita had died. That was it, the only reason he would now speak at length about his experience of the Holocaust. His reason for not speaking to someone sooner came down to his honoring a vow to her that they, individually or together, would not publicly talk about their past. He told me this on the first day we met. He was very calm, even matter-of-fact about it: he could now tell his story because Gita had died, but I had to hurry up and write because he wanted to be with her. Over the next three years, we talked about Gita's insistence they did not talk about their past and he would lean in to me and whisper, "Only to ourselves, in our bedroom, did we remember." He loved telling me that and always had a twinkle in his eye when he did.

A memory of evil and horror, remembered in the most private and intimate surroundings for six decades. How poignant is that?

Lale explained how Gita wanted to put their past behind them, asking him always, how could she have a good and happy life if she kept talking about Birkenau, about losing most of her family? Both Lale and his son, Gary, told me many times how little Gita had ever said in front of Gary; Lale had been more open and up-front with his son about his time as the Tattooist. Yes, both he and Gita had made videos for the USC Shoah Foundation, but their understanding when they agreed to be interviewed was that these tapes would not be readily available to the public.

Other than this interview, Gita had spoken very little of her experience. The friends I met with Lale also confirmed that she did not join in conversations about surviving the Holocaust. They said she listened, just didn't take part or share. Lale admitted to me that he and his male friends spoke about it together, safe in the knowledge they had all shared the same experience and could talk freely among themselves, that no one would judge, that there was no need for shame or guilt within this group. Shabbat dinners after the women had gone to the kitchen to clean up (his words!) became a time to speak of their shared tragedy.

Lale's subsequent desperation to find someone to talk to so soon after Gita's death is testament to how badly he needed to tell the world of the girl whose arm he held, dressed in rags, her head shaven and unbathed, who stole his heart. He also felt if he spoke up and people heard what he had to say, the Holocaust would never happen again. I think he always felt the hand of history on his shoulder, recognized that his role in the Holocaust was unique and worth recording. He was highly intelligent and understood that there was a growing willingness on the part of the remaining generation of survivors to speak out, as they reached the ends of their lives, and a growing need for people to hear and learn from these stories. It was almost as if he felt it was his duty to tell his story before he went to "be with Gita."

I am convinced Lale never intended to reveal the deeply emotional and traumatizing impact of the events he had witnessed and experienced. I think at first he intended to keep that bottled up inside and simply to let me have the facts as he remembered them. Only after he really came to trust me did he allow himself to open up in front of me. Then he would, right up to the end of his life, let slip little bits of stories hidden, buried so deep within that I think he almost surprised himself by speaking them out loud. As I have mentioned before, this was the way I first got to hear about Cilka Klein.

One day we had been out for a coffee (yay!), met several of his friends, and sat with them. They knew by now I was writing Lale's story and with great humor and ribbing were telling me stories of their own and asking him, "Did you tell her [me] that? Bet you never told her about . . ."—generally some mischief the men had gotten up to, resulting in the women present wanting more details. During these informal coffee meetings, I was hearing mostly about Lale and Gita's life in Melbourne, the lifestyle they enjoyed, the parties these friends had been to. When we got back to Lale's apartment, and I had declined a further cup of coffee before he skipped to the kitchen and produced it without asking, I noticed he was in a reflective mood. The giggles and lightness had left him. As we sat down, he turned to me and said, "Did I tell you about Cilka?"

"No, who was she?" I replied.

"She was the bravest person," and wagging his finger at me, he added, "not the bravest girl, the bravest person I ever knew."

When I pushed him to tell me more, he shook his head, turned away from me, head bowed. I could see the trembling lips. I let it go, moved on to a subject less painful—but I could also see that it was a story he wanted, *needed*, me to hear. Gradually over the coming months, he told me about her, always ending his conversation with: "When you have told my story, you must tell Cilka's, I want the world to know about Cilka."

Lale struggled to find the words to describe Cilka's survival in Birkenau. He couldn't or wouldn't use the word "rape." Instead he would say, "He made her do it." When I asked, "Do what?," he squirmed and looked away and muttered, "Sleep with him, you know." Holding his hand above his head, he would say, "He was up here," dropping it down, "She was down here. How could she fight him?" Shaking his head, he would mutter over and over, "There was nothing we could do to help her, save her, from that bastard in Birkenau or what happened to her after." He would then say, "If Gita was here, she could tell you, she would tell you. She visited Cilka in Slovakia after she got out of Siberia, the girls talked about it."

Lale never got to read his story as a novel, but he did get to read it in its original format, a screenplay. After a year, I had a first draft written, and on his birthday, as I sat with him drinking his coffee and eating a small piece of cake he had bought from a local café, I handed him my gift. He ripped the paper off, revealing my bound first draft script of *The Tattooist of Auschwitz*. The cake was pushed aside (he wasn't a big eater anyway) as he flicked through the pages. But he wasn't reading it, he was running his fingers over his and Gita's names on each page. He beamed and giggled—I'll never forget that laugh. It was a wonderful moment for both of us. When I left him that evening, he was still hugging the manuscript close to his chest. It was as if I had given him back a little piece of Gita, written in words—the words he had given to me.

I was lucky to have a local film production company option the script from me. Over the next year, Lale was involved with these people in contributing and developing my original script. All the changes and rewrites were given to him. He offered advice here and there, but he was delighted by the way I had captured his story, in particular by the way I had written about Gita. He had stopped saying, "I need to be with Gita," every time we met. Now he wanted to live for as long as it would take to see their story told to the world.

Sadly, this didn't happen. He died on October 31, 2006—three days after his ninetieth birthday, three years after we first met.

It would not be true to say that through the process of sharing his story Lale lost his pain, trauma, and guilt—he carried so much with him to the end. But I do believe that speaking with me, knowing his story would be told, helped in some way to lighten the burden he'd carried his entire life. I saw firsthand, repeatedly, how talking freely and feeling safe, knowing I would honor his story, helped him reclaim his zest for life.

There were five words Lale would say to me all the time that would have me roll my eyes, and just look at him.

"Did I tell you about . . . ?"

From this opening statement, something I had never heard before might follow. Not helpful when I thought I had a full account of his story and my current draft of his screenplay was being read by others.

He was in a particularly playful mood the day he said, "Did I tell you I was a playboy?"

My initial reaction of mock disapproval had him quickly qualifying how he was referring to his life before Gita. Listening to him tell me about his life as a "playboy" in Bratislava prior to his deportation, with his fine tailored suits, polished shoes, coiffured hair, a physique he was proud of, was a truly joyous experience. He'd had so many girlfriends, he told me. A good job gave him the money to spend on food and wine, entertainment, the designer clothes he craved. As he paced around his living room, he left me, went back to that time and place, describing his life in detail. And what a life! A young man grasping every moment, every opportunity that came his way, he was full of hope for his future. It pleased me to give him the space and safety to talk about his life pre-Auschwitz, a time lost to him. He could never go back to the dream of that bright future; the Holocaust had obliterated those happy times.

I listened in awe to his descriptions of beautiful women and enviable lifestyle, switching my gaze from this excited eighty-eight-year-old man to the photo of Gita on his sideboard. It seemed incongruous that he subsequently fell in love where he did and under the circumstances in which he did. He often told me that he had total belief he would survive Auschwitz-Birkenau and resume his life back in Bratislava. Surely it would be with one of the beautiful women he knew there, whom he hoped to return to? He admitted to me that he didn't necessarily date Jewish girls, that many of his "girlfriends" were not Jewish. Instead he had held the hand of that young girl dressed in rags, and he said, "I knew in that second I could never love another." What was it about Gita that spellbound our playboy? He told me it was her eyes: they were black, they were alive, they bored into him and he couldn't look away. In that terrible place of death, he saw in those eyes a defiance and will to survive.

As Lale opened up more, although I often witnessed his distress, I was also increasingly aware of the effect that telling his story was having in helping him heal. It was a physical and emotional healing for him. To laugh again, connect with his community, go out to movies and cafés with me, shop and cook meals for us both, spend time with my family. And then there was dancing with Tootsie. Him holding that poor dog's front paws in his hands while he swirled around, Tootsie stumbling with him, was, as I told him often, potentially hazardous for a man his age.

He also had this little skip. Whenever he stood up, he would take two steps, skip in the air and click his ankles together. It was six months into our friendship that I first saw "The Skip"—it continued for the rest of his life. I think he allowed me to see the man he was before the Holocaust, perhaps a man he could never quite be with Gita, because of all they had experienced and witnessed together. Perhaps in some way, I helped him become that man again.

As I go forward writing other stories of hope, courage, love, and survival, I will be totally focused once again on caring for the person who is telling me their story, caring for myself, and striving to relate these stories, always honoring those involved and their narrative. It is such a privilege to sit in the homes of ordinary people who have lived through an extraordinary time and be present with them as they take me on a journey through their experiences. In getting to know them and their families, as well as sharing my own story with them, I have made lifelong friendships and my life has been hugely enriched.

Recently, I made a second journey back to Israel, to spend time with the family whose story I tell next. This time I had shekels on me: I was a little wiser about the rules in Israel this time. Meeting this amazing family has been one of the great joys of my life.

The first thing I noticed when I walked into Livia's apartment was the jigsaw puzzle on her dining table. It didn't take long for me to gravitate toward it and tell Livia and her family how much I enjoyed doing puzzles. I use them to shut down from writing. Nothing totally absorbs me like leaning over a thousand tiny pieces of cardboard begging me to put them together, to make something whole out of chaos. Reading a book, watching a movie does not shut my brain down the same way as a jigsaw does. Order out of chaos? Fitting tiny moving pieces into a whole story? I'll leave it to you to figure out what that means.

When I mentioned this to Livia, she immediately agreed. Involuntarily, I picked up a piece and started looking for where it might fit in before realizing what I was doing. "Go ahead," she said. Every member of her family who visits her daily greets her, then they too work on whatever puzzle she has laid out, placing a piece or two before they leave.

A week later, my last few hours with this woman were spent with the two of us sitting opposite each other, trying to outdo one another in placing bits in the puzzle. We talked about our families and how our lives were just like the puzzle in front of us: complicated, but ultimately rewarding. Through this one connection, jigsaw junkies, I got to know this woman on an entirely different level to the person who had survived evil and horror. I saw the calm, steady mind that studied a small piece of a puzzle, held it over the box depicting the scene she was creating, either placed it where it should be or gently put it to one side to be considered again at a later time. Our conversation was about the hope that she has carried for decades of a good life for her children, now extended to her grandchildren and great-grandchildren. She is proud to tell her story, she told me, in the hope that it will make a difference to others. I will be proud to tell her story of hope and resilience. I have said it many times, my books are not my stories: they are Lale's, Cilka's, and these three amazing sisters'.

One thing every survivor has said to me is, "I was lucky." This might sound strange—how is being persecuted for religious faith during the Holocaust lucky?

In April 2018, I was at Auschwitz for the annual March of the Living. Together with thousands of men and women, girls and boys, we marched from Auschwitz to Birkenau. Sitting on the grass on a beautiful spring day, dignitaries and politicians would speak of the need to Never Forget. Never Again.

When the opening music of the formal event ended, the first person to speak was an elderly man. He was dressed in the blue-and-white-striped uniform of this place. The program told me he had been a Polish prisoner here, where I sat, and now lived in the United States. He was helped to the microphone, a granddaughter beside him to support, both emotionally and physically (twice he started to collapse only to be held back up as he insisted on continuing to speak).

I was sitting on the grass examining every blade around me. Did Gita and the other girls sit here, searching for four-leaf clovers? I searched until the words of the old man made me stop and look up at the stage in front of me.

I don't know what I was expecting him to say, probably something about his time here, nearly seventy-five years ago, but he didn't. His opening words were to give thanks and heap praise on the American producer/director Steven Spielberg. He was acknowledging the role Mr. Spielberg had played in keeping the story of the Holocaust alive with his movie *Schindler's List* (1993). On and on he went, urging all of us to give thanks to him—he must have said Mr. Spielberg's name ten times or more.

There is no doubt that that film, among many, continues to keep the Holocaust story alive. I have had the privilege of meeting and sharing a stage with Thomas Keneally, the man who wrote *Schindler's Ark*, the book on which the film is based—in my opinion an Australian hero. However, it is not only this movie that I think of when I think of Mr. Spielberg. It is what he did after making the movie that I believe is Spielberg's greatest achievement in keeping the narrative of the Holocaust alive: the creation of the USC Shoah Foundation.

In sending videographers to far-flung countries to record the individual stories of survivors, he gave voice to them and to their resilience and bravery, giving them an opportunity to tell their story. As many survivors have said to me, there are not two people who would tell the same story. Everyone witnessed and experienced the Holocaust differently. Their own personal backgrounds made them interpret what was happening in a uniquely individual way. No one story is better or more profound than another. Of course, there is an inevitable and terrible similarity in many of the experiences, particularly when it came to witnessing atrocities, but it is the personal suffering that must be acknowledged and told, not just the collective.

Two of the three sisters whose story I tell next went through the same appalling experiences, yet one describes how she was in a "zombie"-like state for most of the time she was in Birkenau. A psychiatrist would describe this as "dissociation," the mind freeing itself from feelings and emotions in order to cope with severe stress or trauma. The other sister—well, she had her eyes wide open. She remembers the small details and is able to describe how she reacted, how she dragged her little sister along with her, looking out for her, caring for her.

I return to the many children and grandchildren who have told me how they want, need, their Holocaust survivor family member to speak out, tell their story, and yet how rare it is for those close to Holocaust survivors to feel able to ask about it, or how often their questions are rebuffed.

I am a mother, a grandmother. I do not believe there is any way I could look into the eyes of my children or grandchildren and tell them of horrors I had lived through. Indeed, I struggled to tell my children of the horrors I heard from Lale Sokolov—I wanted to protect them from secondhand trauma.

Meeting the families of three sisters, Holocaust survivors, in Israel was so uplifting. For the first time, I spent time with first- and second-generation descendants who had grown up hearing every detail of these three brave girls' stories. They told me when they attended survivor children support groups, they were envied because these women had chosen to speak about their experiences. The love which exuded from every family member toward each other was palpable. I believe their love for each other and family was due to the honesty and openness their parents had demonstrated with them, telling them their stories at age-appropriate times and in age-appropriate language.

It was obvious to me this family had healed from the trauma their parents had experienced. Their painful past was never to be forgotten, it was to be talked about often and shared. Now, that's courage.

It must always be the individual's choice what to talk about and what they choose to take to their grave. Thankfully, Steven Spielberg has ensured that thousands of survivor testimonies now exist, and the individual stories of the Holocaust need never be forgotten. These videos offer hope to those who made them, and to us, that through the darkest times in history, people clung to each other and hoped by their survival to tell generations of the hope they carried. Hope is the last thing to die. In fact, as that terminally ill young woman told her mother in hospital: "It takes only moments to die, the rest of the time we are living."

With every breath we take, we are living.

When I chose to fictionalize Lale's story, I wanted to tell it the way he told it to me. I was telling *his* story, not my version of it, and so I stayed true to his storytelling, honoring his narrative in re-creating his experiences. The only thing I couldn't re-create was his charming Eastern European accent and how he would get words back to front or jumbled up in a way that would have us both laughing. He was very ready to laugh at himself. Not having a deadline meant there was no pressure for either of us, no time limit on his telling and my listening.

Taking time to really listen to someone and hear their story requires patience and perseverance. Several years ago, I read an article about the upcoming Olympic Games. The article was about the cost of security to protect the athletes and officials. The last paragraph mentioned the 1956 Olympic Games in Melbourne and the small security team back then. The head of security had been only twenty-three years old at the time. Fascinated by this story, and wanting to learn more, I did a quick calculation and guessed the man might still be alive. After calling every man with that name in Melbourne, I finally struck gold. I asked the elderly gentleman on the other end of the phone if I could come and talk to him about his time at the Games in 1956. I was told he had no intention of talking about that time, Official Secrets Act and all that, but I kept him talking long enough to wangle a coffee out of him.

Lale had died and I now had my Sundays free. For nearly a year, I had coffee two to three times a month with this man, who had been the head of security at the 1956 Olympic Games. We enjoyed each other's company, the coffee was much better than Lale's, but he was teasing me and giving me very little.

One day, out of the blue he called to say his health was failing and he wanted to tell me all. I arranged with the curator of the venue where the Games were held to have access, and with my children acting as a film crew, we spent several hours recording his story. They were known as the "Friendly Games," but they were held at the height of the Cold War, around the time of the Soviet invasion of Hungary and the Suez Canal crisis. Lies, spies, murder, and abductions were the reality. This one man was front and center of it all. He saw the abductions, sat with the politicians who scrambled to cover up what was going on in our town. A screenplay exists of this story; it sits in the bottom drawer of my desk. Maybe one day, it will see the light of day.

Like Lale, this man experienced a form of therapeutic release in telling his story. I got to spend many more wonderful moments with him before he died. I also got to hear his story of life after the Games, and like Lale, it was his love for his wife and their family he especially wanted to tell me about. As I got to spend time with his wife every time I visited—truth to tell, it was she who made the great coffee—I understood his initial reluctance to talk to me. He had lived the most amazing life with the people he loved surrounding him, with no need to look back, but as is so often the case, he chose to speak out toward the end. I chose to listen, and I am the richer for knowing him and hearing his story.

The world is a big place; your community and neighborhood are small in comparison. Stories like the ones I have told are around us all the time, among the people we live with. If you are that way inclined, if you feel your life might be enriched by meeting people outside your circle, spending time with them, listening to their stories, you might find it changes your life—just look around you.

7

Cilka's Story—Listening to History

When *The Tattooist of Auschwitz* was published, I began to receive letters from all over the world. People wrote, telling me how much they loved Lale and Gita's story, but many of them also asked the question: "What happened to Cilka?" People wanted to know and I wanted to tell them. I needed to keep my promise to Lale to write Cilka Klein's story—the novel that became *Cilka's Journey*.

I had done my research: I had spoken to survivors who knew Cilka in Birkenau and I had also engaged a professional researcher in Moscow to find all the documents and information she could about Vorkuta Gulag, the "corrective labor camp" Cilka was sent to at the end of the war. What I didn't have were details of Cilka's life in Slovakia, both before Auschwitz and after her release from Siberia. I had Lale's own testimony and my friendship with him to inform my story of his and Gita's lives; I only had other people's recollections about Cilka. I wanted to get to know her better. I wanted to find out where she was from, to walk where she would have walked. I needed to listen to her history firsthand.

I had visited Slovakia on several occasions. My wonderful researchers—no, *friends*—from Lale's hometown of Krompachy had arranged people for me to meet, places to visit, documents to look at in my search to learn all I could about the girl called Cilka. Stopping off in London, I was joined by my publisher, Margaret, and together, we flew into Kosice.

Picked up by the mayor of Krompachy's driver, Peter, we were driven to the town hall at Krompachy to be met by the mayor, deputy mayor, and the two women who had been acting on my behalf, trying to uncover details of Cilka. Anna, Krompachy's historian, a woman well into her seventies, but with the agility and enthusiasm of someone much younger, greeted me with a warm embrace. We had first met in Auschwitz over a year earlier. She and twenty-five others from Lale's hometown traveled there when they heard I was to attend the March of the Living, but that's another story. With Anna was Lenka, her daughter-in-law, a beautiful young woman who had lived in Ireland for fifteen years. Listening to her speak both English and Slovakian with the most beautiful Irish accent was a delight.

In the mayor's office, Margaret was introduced to Slivovitz. I had met the plum brandy before, we were old friends now—and I both feared and looked forward to being reacquainted. The first sip, as always, seared my throat, took my breath away, but tasted so much better as the shot was then swallowed the way it was meant to be—in one gulp! Coffee and cake were also on offer and countered some of the effects of the alcohol. We all went for a walk around the town, stopping off at the Holocaust memorial we had jointly pledged to fund. From there it was on to a local restaurant, where Margaret was introduced to Slovakian cuisine.

Our friend Slivovitz had accompanied us to eat.

Driven back to Kosice that night, I fell asleep easily. The next morning, we were picked up by Peter,

Anna, and Lenka. We knew the name of the town where Cilka was born: Sabinov. We also knew the name of the town where she and her family were taken from on their fateful journey to Auschwitz: Bardejov.

Lenka had done an amazing job in gaining access to documents relating to Cilka's birth details. From Holocaust databases, we had found an entry for her and we were certain we had identified her father and a sister. Only by seeing her birth record could we be certain of her family connections, though.

At the town hall in Sabinov, we left Peter to park the car, and Lenka, Anna, Margaret, and I ventured in. Down this corridor, up another, around several corners, we eventually knocked on the door of the bureaucrat designated to show us Cilka's birth record. She sat behind a large desk, two chairs on the other side. In front of her was a large bound ledger with a beautiful aged leather cover. Lenka and I sat down in the two seats as she turned the book around to show us the entry we sought. The first thing that struck me was the large sheets of white paper covering up the entries above and below Cilka's. I accepted the need for privacy of the others whose names appeared on the page—their privacy was complete with me, as I could not read a word of Slovakian.

Anna and Margaret leaned over our shoulders as Lenka read out the details and I looked on in wonder. My request to bring out my mobile phone and take a picture was quickly rebuffed. Lenka read out the details while Anna wrote them down—we had been given permission to do this:

17th March 1926
Cecilia [Cilka is a diminutive for Cecilia]
Girl
Father Mikulas Klein—Jew—28 years
Mother Fani Blech—Jew—22 years

Beautiful copperplate handwriting recorded the intimate details of Cilka's birth. Immediately, we recognized her father's name as being the person in the databases we had found. Now we learned her mother's name was Fani. Both their dates of birth were recorded, and her father's nationality was listed as Hungarian. At the far end of the record something had been written in another hand, another pen—this we ignored initially as we took in the information before us.

With Lenka translating, we told the bureaucrat about Cilka and the book I was writing. Initially, she had been rather frosty, but then she started asking questions, becoming engaged in the story of Cilka. When she asked us if we would like to see if she could find the record of Cilka's parents' marriage, a chorus of "Yes, please" resounded in the room. She only had to go to the cupboard on a far wall to look for the book of marriages that would have the records around the time we presumed Mikulas and Fani had married.

As she turned to the cupboards behind her, I quickly moved the white pieces of paper covering the other entries aside. Back and forward, I flicked pages, scanning each one, looking to see if any other birth record had anything added to the original entry as Cilka's had. But I saw none. I asked Lenka to read out the additional entry and was glad I was sitting down when she did so: the notation recorded that Cecilia Klein had presented to this office in Sabinov in 1958 a document from the government in Bratislava declaring her to be a citizen of the State of Czechoslovakia.

Up until this moment I had been bothered by a discrepancy we had identified in the databases recording survivors and victims of the Holocaust. Cilka had been listed as "Murdered in Auschwitz," something which I knew from Lale was not true. She had survived both Auschwitz-Birkenau and Vorkuta Gulag and had returned and lived the rest of her life in Kosice, Slovakia. Cilka and Gita stayed in touch after they moved to Australia and Gita had visited Cilka on more than one occasion when she made a trip back to Slovakia with their son, Gary. But here was actual written proof that she had survived. Cilka had made the effort to come to the town where she was born and have her birth record amended. Why would she have done this, we wondered. Perhaps it was because she needed to prove her identity in order to either get a job or get married—we know she did both.

"I've found it!" the bureaucrat said and she lifted another large book onto the desk, turning it around for us to look at. This time she was relaxed, not bothering to cover up other names, sharing in our excitement.

What we read was this: on June 10, 1919, Mikulas Klein married Cecilia Blech—Cecilia, not Fani, who was listed as Cilka's mother. Then the ever-diligent Margaret made a comment regarding the date of their marriage and the date of Cilka's birth: there was a seven-year gap. While today, you wouldn't question a couple not starting a family for seven years after their marriage, it seemed unusual for the early twentieth century. She asked the bureaucrat if we could look back through the birth records to see if we could find any other children born to Mikulas and Fani.

On August 23, 1924, Magdalena had been born to the couple. Mikulas had proudly signed the book registering his newborn daughter. We continued to turn the pages. On December 28, 1921, Olga was born to Mikulas, but here, the mother's name was given as Cecilia. This was the first time Mikulas had proudly registered his firstborn daughter.

While excited to learn that Cilka had two older sisters, we were perplexed as to why the name Cecilia was registered as the mother of Olga, but it was switched to Fani for Magdalena and Cilka. We went back and looked at Cilka's record and there we saw it was not Mikulas who had registered her, but her grandmother, Roza Weisz. We subsequently learned that Mikulas's first wife, Cecilia, died four months after giving birth to Olga. He then married Cecilia's sister Fani, the mother of Magdalena and Cilka—this would have been a regular occurrence in those times. We can only wonder why Cilka's grandmother registered her birth, but she gave this grandchild the name of her dead daughter.

The pieces of the jigsaw were fitting together.

Next stop, Bardejov, where we knew the family

had moved at some point after Cilka's birth and from where we knew they boarded a train bound for Auschwitz. "It's just an hour away," Lenka told Margaret and me when we asked how long it would take to get there. The eastern Slovakian towns of Krompachy, Sabinov, Bardejov, and Vranov—all towns I am now familiar with—are only an hour away from Kosice and an hour away from each other.

Once again, Lenka had worked her magic and the education authorities in Bardejov had agreed we could see Cilka's last two years' school records. Again, we entered and encountered a suspicious bureaucrat clutching a large journal. Our identifications were requested, shown, taken away, and I presume copied. Only then was the book put down and opened for us to see.

Once again, a bureaucrat got caught up in the story of Cilka and before we knew it, she was looking through the book to find the school reports of Magdalena and Olga. Tentatively, I asked if I could photograph the reports and this time I was given permission. Margaret and I reached for our phones and clicked away. Lenka and Anna translated the reports. We learned so much: a bright girl, Cilka excelled at gymnastics and mathematics. Their religion was noted—Israelites. Mikulas's occupation was given as driver and handyman.

Leaving the building, back out into the heat and bright sunshine, we only had to walk a few hundred meters down the same street to stand outside the home Cilka and her family lived in—until the day they didn't.

As we walked toward the address, the street was empty, probably because it was extremely hot, and no sane person should have been outside. As we approached the house, we could hear music coming from a radio of some kind, accompanied by voices singing along.

I deliberately chose to approach the house from the opposite side of the street, wanting to take in the building in its entirety: see its roof, the outline of the windows and doors. From the other side of the road I was able to see the singers—two workmen replacing timber in the house next to Cilka's. Anna whispered that they were singing a Ukrainian folk song. She reminded us we were not far from the Ukrainian border and that people in Bardejov would speak that language along with Hungarian and possibly Polish. Once again, I was embarrassed at my lack of languages. I so admired my multilingual companions. I also finally understood how Cilka would have managed in Vorkuta—she would have had a good working knowledge of Russian.

I took in Cilka's house, a soft pastel-green cottage with white-framed windows and door, proudly maintained, opening directly onto the cobbled street. Above the front door two dormer windows provided the eyes for the occupants to look down on the street. I wondered if one of these had been Cilka's bedroom. Along from the front door double wooden doors were set back from the street. These would have led to the courtyard behind the house.

I touched the door leading into the house. A new door, it would not have been the door Cilka and her family opened to enter the sanctuary that was home to them. Did they hold out hope that one day they would return?

I think Cilka did.

The walk to the synagogue was energy-sapping in the heat with no shade en route. We were met by a member of the Bardejov Jewish Preservation Committee. He would be showing us the old and new (1950s) synagogue. As we walked toward the small, simple new building, we heard beautiful, haunting music coming from within. We walked inside, up to the doors leading into the prayer room, then stopped at the entrance, frozen as the music wrapped itself around us and we gazed upon a choir of some twenty young boys and girls with an accompanying quartet, singing with the purest voices that reverberated off the walls and landed deep within my chest.

Instinctively, both Margaret and I reached out to each other, our hands meeting, our eyes fixed on the vision in front of us. I felt the tears slowly roll down my cheeks. When the song was finished, I watched as Margaret wiped tears from her eyes. Lenka and Anna embraced us as the emotion of what we had stumbled on took effect. They were singing a Slovakian love song, Anna told us.

We stayed to hear one more song, ignored by the musicians. Our guide was wanting to move us on and so we followed him upstairs to a small gallery area. Here, we were shown photographs, paintings done by small children—the only remnants of a Jewish community in Bardejov prior to 1942.

Outside, we took the ten or so steps that connected us to the old synagogue. I was expecting to find it dark inside but on opening the door, we were greeted by blinding light. Part of the roof was missing, and the summer sun shone down into the ruins. Part of the floor was also missing, the dirt visible below the broken boards that remained. Pushed into one corner stood a few remaining pews. We looked up to the balcony where Cilka, her mother, and her sisters would have sat while her father prayed below. A shattered building marking shattered lives, yet it still held the spiritual power once offered to many.

There was one more place to visit. Behind a locked gate we entered a garden with green grass, colorful flowers, and a marble wall. We walked along the wall looking for the names we hoped we wouldn't find, but we did. Here were listed the names of the Jewish people from Bardejov who did not survive the Holocaust. Here, we found the names of Cilka, her two sisters, and her father. Like the Holocaust databases we have searched, Cilka is listed as not having survived. There was no record of her mother and we have been unable to ascertain what became of her. Lale told me Cilka was the only member of her immediate family to survive the Holocaust, that her father was sent to the gas chamber immediately on arriving at Auschwitz and her sisters and mother died later. Other testimonies I have read and listened to about Cilka confirm this.

As we were driven by Peter the one hour back to our hotel in Kosice, Margaret and I said very little.

We were each lost in thought as we processed all we had learned, all we had seen. I struggled to separate my elation at having discovered something of Cilka's early life from my overwhelming sense of grief for the lives lost and the pain and trauma endured by so many for so long. I had stood outside a beautiful home, but its beauty was tarnished by knowing what had happened to its rightful owners.

There was one last thing to do on that trip before it was time to fly back to Australia. I had been asked by the owner of a bookstore in Kosice if I could talk to some locals one afternoon in his store. I said yes and over fifty people turned up and squeezed into the lovely interior. The translator struggled at times, so people in the audience began to help him and it became one big, loud conversation.

I was talking about Lale's story; Cilka's was still a work in progress. As I ended my talk, I told them I was in Kosice researching my next book, *Cilka's Journey*. An elderly man sitting midway in the crowd put his hand up and asked, "Is it about Cecilia Kovacova?" (He used her married name.) I pounced on him, said yes, it was, and did he know her? He told me he was her neighbor and that he would like to speak to me about her.

We sat on stools—Michael, Margaret, the translator, and me. Michael, a tiny, stooped gentleman with fierce blue eyes burning with life, sat down with me. He told me about living in the same apartment building as Cilka for many decades; how they were the only Jewish people in the building. He told me how he and Cilka acknowledged each other as fellow survivors, but in secret—the Holocaust was not to be discussed under Communism. He wanted us to hear his story: he was a hidden child, surviving the Holocaust by being passed from family to family in the nearby Tatra Mountains. He and Cilka had talked about visiting Israel together, but neither of them ever did. It was an enormous privilege to meet him and hear his story.

I use the words "I am so humbled" often. That's because I am truly humbled to have been able to tell the stories I have, to have met and spoken with so many people around the world. I hope I have honored Cilka in telling her story, as I promised Lale I would. I am humbled to have had that privilege.

8

The Cost of Listening

Sometimes we don't need advice. We just need somebody to listen to us.

"He's fine." My stock answer to my family's question "How is Lale?" on my return from visiting him, six months or so into our friendship.

Lale Sokolov had met my family, flirted with my young adult daughter, joked with my husband that I might be his wife, but I was Lale's girlfriend. My three young adult children and my husband had grown to love this charming old rascal, so they all registered that this was a major shift in my response to their eagerly awaited update on Lale and the stories he was telling me.

When I'd first introduced Lale into our lives, I'd often arrive home as dinner was being served and the meal was consumed as I shared the antics of his doggies along with snippets of what we had talked about—when I say "snippets," I never really shared the details, but I'd give a sense of what we'd discussed. And now they got just two words: "He's fine." I was pushing them away, but I was also aware that my family was watching me carefully, concerned but unsure about what should be done.

The shift in my response to my family coincided with my acceptance into Lale's circle by his doggies and the switch in his approach to sharing with me the emotional pain and deep suffering of his time at Auschwitz-Birkenau. As I've said, at first, Lale had talked about his life in a clinical, factual way. He told me he had a brother and sister, and a little about his parents, but nothing about his childhood that told me anything about how he became Lale the man. He described Auschwitz and Birkenau to me so vividly that when I visited there in 2018 for the first time, I knew where to look for the block he lived in, for the one Gita lived in, for the spot where he worked near the gas chamber/crematoria. But in those early meetings he didn't tell me how he felt walking through this hell on earth. I knew there was more, and that it was deeply distressing to him, but I could also sense that he wanted to tell me about it. He would start to say something, then stop and pull back. Pursing his lips, he would drop his head to his chest, one hand seeking out one of his doggies to pat. His actions revealed the pain and anguish he carried deep down. As I've described, it was only when I introduced him to my family and made myself vulnerable to him that I established a proper empathetic connection. With that came trust and the beginnings of what became true friendship.

That level of trust—symbolized by Tootsie giving me the ball—was an enormous honor, but it came with an emotional burden that I struggled with. Looking back, I should have seen the signs earlier, should have known what was going on, because of my job in the social work department, but it's always easier to see what's going on in others than in ourselves. In the caring professions it's often said that the practitioners "talk the talk" but forget to "walk the walk." Regular, structured supervision is crucial for workers in mental health. In my job at the hospital, what we called "informal mini-debriefs" also helped immensely. We knew we could always seek out a colleague to listen to us for a few minutes as we talked through a troubling situation, not even necessarily to comment or provide advice—just to listen.

My tears flowed as Lale told me stories so evil and horrible I struggled to comprehend them. Listening to his description of man's inhumanity to man, of what the person sitting beside me—and so many others—had suffered, I would experience a visceral, physically painful feeling deep in my chest. At times, I struggled to control my breathing. Other times, it was as though my hearing had shut down: I would look at Lale and see his lips moving but hear nothing. In *The Body Keeps the Score*, Bessel van der Kolk, MD, a world authority on trauma, describes how our reaction to trauma isn't only mental, it is powerfully physiological. I was experiencing a "fight or flight" response to what I was hearing, what is known as experiencing vicarious trauma, and I was then "dissociating" to protect myself from what I was hearing. My brain was shutting down in order to try to manage my physical reactions.

I would snap myself out of my subconscious trance and try to focus—in time, as I've said, I learned to copy Lale and put my hand down and stroke the heads of his doggies, in order to bring myself back into the room. It was at times like this that I wished I had a pad and pen in front of me to distract myself by writing down the words I was hearing. Try this, it works: write down the words someone is saying to you while they are talking. Even if you are a super-fast writer and get every word down, the emotional impact of what you are being told is never as strong as it is if you listen fully and without distraction. Not even close. You are hearing but not really "listening" to what you are being told. It's a powerful distancing tool and one that can be useful.

But I knew I had to really listen to Lale, hear what he was telling me—that was my privilege and my responsibility. As I've said, from the first day I met him, I had deliberately not brought any recording material with me. No paper and pen or a recording machine. I knew from my experience at work that people talk freely when they know they have your undivided attention, and I had noticed this was particularly the case with older people. So often when talking to an elderly person I saw how impatient they were to tell what they wanted someone to hear. They always reacted strongly to being interrupted. I remember on one occasion interrupting someone because I wanted more details about something she had just said. She snapped at me and told me to shut up and listen. She must have seen my eyes widening and my "Are you serious?" look. Her response—"Do you know how hard it is to get someone to listen to you when you're my age? Nobody wants to hear what I have to say—you would think I was invisible! Now please, just listen to me because I'm going to tell you what I want you to hear, right here and now."

That brief exchange told me everything I needed to know about listening to the elderly. All too often they are invisible, and even if they are seen and acknowledged, we do not expect to hear anything from them that can help our lives. We don't listen, don't ask.

How wrong we are.

Early on in our conversations I had discovered that Lale got frustrated if I interrupted him with a question while he was talking. The pause in his flow was enough of a distraction to make it difficult to get back to what he'd been telling me. It's not that he would get angry with me, but clearly, he did not appreciate being interrupted and he'd become confused in his narrative and often give up soon afterward. It often seemed to me that Lale had rehearsed what he wanted to tell me in advance. He knew when I would be visiting, either after work or on a Sunday afternoon. It was obvious he had spent time, either that day or the previous one, deciding what he would talk about. He would launch straight into a story with very little chitchat. Not that it mattered. My biggest challenge in not writing or recording was trying to remember the names and titles of the SS and prisoner functionaries. Then there was the small problem of Lale sometimes slipping back into his native tongue of Slovakian, or German, or Russian.

As part of writing this book, I've been rereading the notes I would frantically type up within hours of leaving Lale each time, anxious to get it all down before I forgot. I have been entertained by my initial attempts to write down the names and titles he used and grateful to the internet and the books I read, the experts I consulted, for helping me to identify people and places. I see once more his immaculate living and dining room, the painting of the Gypsy woman, his doggies Tootsie and Bam Bam greeting me at the door, chasing a tennis ball, curled up asleep under the table we often sat at. I taste Lale's famously bad coffee. I savor the sweet taste of the wafer biscuits he served me. I see the packet, see the Hebrew writing that he loved to joke I couldn't read. I look over the notes I carefully made about his mental state and mine and I can feel, as if it were yesterday, my anxiety and the sense of responsibility I felt to this man. And then I think back to more recent memories, of sitting in Israel with ninety-two-year-old Livia, who served me those same wafer biscuits.

They still taste wonderful.

The time I spent with Livia, and the brief time I spent with her sister Magda, hearing them talk about their past, was vastly different from being with Lale. In the case of the sisters, members of their families were also present and took part in the conversations, sometimes contributing, reminding Livia and Magda of incidents the sisters had skipped over. The three sisters had told their stories so often, and in such detail, that as I listened, it occurred to me that, shocking as it was, the fact that they had shared their trauma with their wider family had created a narrative of survival and hope out of their dark history.

I can only speak from my own direct experience, but during my visit to Israel, I never felt I had to distance myself from the pain and trauma these women had endured, as I had with Lale. Oh, it was still there, still played out on their faces. I still felt the need to reach out and touch Livia's hand, reassure her I was listening to her, acknowledge I was hearing the pain and toll her story was taking on her, particularly when she spoke about her mother and grandfather and her life as a child. Contrast this with Lale and Gita, who relived their pain and trauma, for the most part, alone.

History and memory. Taste and sound. The elements that remind us we live, we have lived, we love, we have loved, we are loved. In my case I continue to live, to love and be loved in return. It is these connections that ultimately gave me the strength to be open to what I was hearing from Lale, to honor it.

My husband and children continued to ask why I didn't want to talk about my time with Lale and why I was becoming more distracted and withdrawn on my return home after each visit. I evaded their questions as best I could with the lame excuse that there was no need for them to know the details of the horror he had experienced and witnessed. He was fine; I was fine. They pressed me about it for several weeks and I saw the looks they exchanged.

I am confident I didn't take any of Lale's trauma into my workplace and let it affect the people I interacted with there. Of course, my colleagues might say differently. I do believe I was very good at separating out my work life from my personal life, only ever telling each cohort what I wanted them to know about the other life I lived.

I recall a colleague coming to me one day, saying she had a patient on her ward who had numbers on her arm. She wanted to know if she should ask about them. Again, no expert, but I told her, "Ask away, she will either want to talk to you about them, or not— her decision." She did ask and had a long conversation with the patient about her time in Auschwitz. My colleague told me she thought talking about the numbers helped them both. The patient had a non-threatening, not emotionally connected person to talk to; my colleague was enlightened about one person's survival.

My family members weren't the only people in my life who knew about my friendship with Lale. I had shared much of my time with him and his Holocaust story with my work colleagues, who were interested that I had befriended this man who represented "living history." In my acknowledgments in

The Tattooist of Auschwitz, I thank my former boss, Glenda Bawden. If it wasn't for her support in understanding how important my time with Lale was, I'm not sure I would be writing this today. Many times, I went to her asking for an hour or two here and there to go and see him, to take him to the movies, to respond to one of his "Where have you been, have you written my book yet?" calls. She understood the path grief can take and she would give me the "nod" that said, "Off you go."

There were one or two others I confided in too, also social workers at the hospital, dedicated to making a difference to patients and their families during tragic and traumatic times. One day, I was having a chat with a colleague who had also become a friend. Answering my phone, I dropped my head in my hands. While I loved hearing Lale's delightful Eastern European accent, this time when I heard him ask, "Where have you been?" a pit of anxiety formed in my stomach and I felt suddenly overwhelmed. How long had it been since we had spent time together? I suddenly couldn't think, my mind was a blank. Lale immediately answered the question. "It's been two weeks since you came. When are you coming to see me?" *Two weeks*. I was not aware it had been so long. We had been seeing each other one to three times a week. I immediately promised to come and see him when I finished work that day, my anxiety now coupled with a powerful feeling of guilt.

When I hung up, my very observant colleague asked, "What's wrong?"

With the comfort that comes of speaking to someone you have known and respected for several years, I said it was hard for me to spend long periods with Lale, listening to him tell me of so much evil and horror. It was a combination of being unable fully to comprehend the details of what I was hearing with the knowledge that this evil had been his reality for nearly three years. My colleague listened as I poured out my feelings of anger, fear that I was pulling away from my family because I didn't want to share such terrible stories with them. I told her I was worried that I was causing Lale too much pain and possible harm, and that I realized I was now displaying physical symptoms of stress myself.

She asked me whether I felt he was becoming dependent upon me and my place in his life. I couldn't say for sure that was the case, but he did seem faintly reproachful whenever he thought there had been too big a gap since we'd last seen each other. And the phone call she had just witnessed wasn't the first time he had called me at work. He always asked straightaway: "Where have you been?" Never, "Hello, how are you?"

When she asked me how Lale had changed since we first met, I had to admit it was obvious to me he had transitioned from the stabbing pain of new grief at losing Gita, and that I had begun to hear him laugh occasionally. That laugh—more a giggle than a laugh—was music to my ears. He had also developed a little skip whenever he stood up. I had even caught him dancing with Tootsie, holding her up by her front paws.

"So," she said, "Lale is giggling, skipping around, and dancing with his dog, while you're feeling depressed and anxious, unable to discuss this with your family, and at some level possibly putting off spending time with him. What do you think is going on here?"

I muttered something about perhaps not being the best person to have accepted his request to listen and tell his story, that it was too much for me to cope with, that I wasn't sure I could do justice to it, I was busy with work and my family. As I was mumbling in my "poor me" moment, my colleague snapped me back to reality. "Really, Heather," she said firmly. "You are experiencing a classic case of transference or vicarious trauma. Recognize it, deal with it, find a strategy that works for you to move on. You know you have no right to own any part of his pain, grief, or trauma, it's not yours."

Her words smacked me in the face. This wasn't supposed to happen to me. I knew all of this stuff, how had I allowed it to happen? I had met a stranger who had a story he wanted to tell someone. Someone who wasn't Jewish. We had spent many months together getting to know each other. His story was playing out into a story I was writing on my computer. My research was teaching me what my small-town New Zealand education had not—the level of inhumanity and evil that was the Holocaust.

Listening deeply to someone else's traumatic experiences comes with dangers, as I was discovering. Anyone carrying out therapeutic work must learn to monitor themselves for signs of vicarious trauma and often the first signs are physical, as mine were: racing heart, the sick feeling in the pit of my stomach, those moments when I seemed to disappear from the room. This was my body keeping the score. What can go with this often is a feeling of guilt. I hadn't lived through that terrible time, so I was suppressing my feelings, and in doing so, becoming overwhelmed by them. It was time to walk the walk and practice some self-care. I knew I didn't want to give up on telling Lale's story—he and I had come so far already, and our connection was real. I also knew, when I really thought about it, that I could cope with what I was hearing, that it wasn't too much for me, provided I found ways to manage myself.

Immediately after this conversation, I started thinking of strategies to counter the transference of pain and trauma I was experiencing. Some of them had merit, others were unrealistic, like asking Lale to answer preprepared questions so I could control his storytelling. There was no way I could do that. Equally, I didn't want to find someone else to listen to him. I knew he had "chosen" me, that what we had was very special, that I had the resilience to make this work.

My colleague asked what it was that worried me most about the distress I was experiencing in being with Lale. It didn't take me long to answer—I knew exactly what it was. What gave me greatest anxiety was my mood on returning home to my family each time I had been with him. It was one thing for me to have internalized a pain and grief I wasn't entitled to, another to let it play out with my family, who had no idea how I was feeling as I "protected" them, or so I thought, from Lale's pain. I had become closed and withdrawn in a way they had never experienced before. I was selfishly not allowing them to assist me through this period, not giving them the chance to comfort me and share the emotional toll I was carrying alone, telling myself I was protecting them. In retrospect, it was simply an extension of my not sharing the tragedy and trauma I listened to at work every day. I didn't recognize that it was different here: they knew Lale personally and felt invested in his story, as I did, whereas the people I met on a daily basis at work were unknown to them, and I approached the "day job" in a professional way that enabled me to cope. With Lale, I was paying an incredibly high price for not separating out those two very different experiences.

So how did I do it? Lale lived on the first floor of an apartment block overlooking the street. I was always guaranteed a parking space right outside his building. He loved to joke every time I left him that he would "see me to my car." As we kissed goodbye at his front door and I made my way down the stairs, the small path that connected to the road, he and the doggies went out onto his balcony, where he would lean over to wave me off, telling me to drive safely. I always thought this was ironic, given I had only let him drive me somewhere once, which ended with my declaring I still had a lot of life to live and I was behind the wheel from now on. As I drove away, he would still be waving from his balcony. He never knew that from that day on, I drove the two hundred meters to a small side street, where I would park and sit quietly with my thoughts, or merely clear my head, making the separation between Lale and my family. I called it "centering myself." Sometimes I would reach for my go-to CD, then close my eyes and lose myself. It was, and still is, the soundtrack to my favorite movie— *Out of Africa*. I always knew when the moment felt right to turn the ignition and go home to my family, be the wife and mother I wanted, needed, to be. Just as importantly, I was able to once again look forward to my return to Lale and his doggies.

I learned, as I have said, to reach down and put my hand on one of the doggies' heads whenever I needed to center myself with Lale, when what he was telling me threatened to engulf us both. I'd pull myself back into that lovely, orderly room and that beautiful man, my friend. I learned when it was time to stop and move on to a safer subject. I'd try to get him to tell me a positive story about life after the war by way of balance, and as I was driving away, I'd think about that. I was careful not to imagine the awful things he told me about happening to me, or members of my family. Always, I pictured it happening to others, to him and Gita and Cilka—but almost to a different version of Lale than the man I knew now. I thought of it in terms of the story I was creating and told myself over and over again that Lale and Gita and Cilka had survived, made lives for themselves, found happiness after the war. Their stories had an ending beyond the Holocaust, and it was *their* stories I was telling, not the story of the horror of that time.

And so I opened up to my family, explained to them that Lale was telling me details of his survival that were horrific, painful for him to talk about. We agreed I would tell them some stories, but they were happy for me to determine what those stories would be. It was enough for them to know I was making it possible for him to safely open up and talk about his past, and that I was able to deal with the emotional impact of those stories. I would talk to them freely about my time with him, if not the content of our conversations. I also spoke to my colleagues at the hospital, who were endlessly supportive and practical. If I hadn't had them then I would have sought counseling—often an essential part of dealing with any experience of trauma, lived or vicarious.

Practical Tips to Counter
the Cost of Listening

Just to recap, here are some key things that we must all learn to do when we are listening to people who have experienced trauma:

- Be aware of your own response—remember, sometimes your head tells you everything is fine, but you notice that you are shaking, your heart is racing. This is your body having the emotional response for you—act on that.

- Use a ritual to "ground" yourself, to shake off what you've just heard and return to your personal life. Mine was parking the car around the corner from Lale and then the drive home, which separated me from the experience.

- Be careful never to picture yourself or a loved one in the experience. Instead, create a cartoon version, a character of the person speaking, taking you through the experience.

- As my friend and colleague said to me, what you are hearing is not your story, you have no right to take it on.

- Keep yourself grounded in the everyday, know who your people are, who's got your back.
- Find someone to talk to—all therapists have a therapist, in a system known as supervision, to ensure they have an objective soundboard for the work they are doing.
- Pick your time of day. Try not to put yourself into the role of being a listener when you are hungry/tired/have had a busy day. In hindsight, my visits with Lale often came after an incredibly busy day at the hospital. I enjoyed them better and felt more able to cope when I saw him at weekends.
- Practice self-care—we should all do this, and we all know it, but often we don't. Make sure your life is balanced between work and play. Socialize. Exercise. Eat well. Don't drink too much—especially if you find you are using alcohol as a coping mechanism.

Conclusion

Stories of hope have sustained humankind since the dawn of time, handed down from generation to generation, passed on to friends, shared with strangers. They are the last thing that will die in each of us.

I have been lucky enough to have listened to thousands of stories of hope over the last few years. People want me to know how Lale's, Gita's, and Cilka's courage and love sustains them and how these people, who survived such tragedy and trauma, have encouraged them to try to live the best life they can. They may not have realized they were telling me their own stories of hope or how many times they used the word *hope*, but it is that word that jumps out at me as I read their emails and letters, or listen to the stories shared with me at book events all over the world.

It is not every day I get an email from an official working in a prison. Truth be told, it has only happened once. It resulted in an experience that will stay with me forever. This prison had a small library for the 1,500 inmates. I was told a handful of prisoners had read my book and started sharing their version of Lale with other prisoners, who in turn were sharing it with fellow prisoners. The official wanted me to know he had never seen a book have such an impact. I won't provide further details, in order to protect the privacy of the men I visited.

Traveling there with my publicist, we went through all the necessary security inspections, had everything but the clothes we were wearing taken from us, before being escorted into the library. The shelves had been pushed aside and, in the center, square plastic cubes were placed for the men to sit on.

The inmates soon sauntered in, all calling out greetings, wanting to fist-bump me; a few shook my hand, but the majority wanted the fist bump. I had planned a structured talk. That didn't happen. For the next two hours, we chatted informally. The men were talking between themselves about Lale; sometimes I was just talking to a handful of them while other conversations went on nearby. What they were sharing was their personal lives outside of prison and the significant others they wanted to get back to, in order to live a good life like Lale and Gita's. One man said: "That dude Lale had a prison way worse than ours," and off they went, comparing the two experiences. They laughed; some wept and were comforted by the man sitting next to them.

My publishers had sent along copies of *The Tattooist of Auschwitz* for the men. Taking their copies, they came up to ask me to sign them. Someone had to find a pen for me; mine was somewhere at the front of the prison with my handbag. The first few men gave me their names and I dedicated the book to them. Then a young man handed me his book, and when I asked him his name, he said he couldn't read or write. He asked me if I would dedicate the book to his mum and add the words "I promise, Mum, I will never come back inside again." The men lining up behind him heard this. For the next hour, I dedicated books, not to the men standing before me, but to the most important people in their lives on the outside—I didn't even try to hold it together.

"To my daughter, she's sixteen, tell her how proud

Daddy is that she has a job interview." "To my wife, tell her I'm sorry she's bringing the kids up on her own." "To my partner," and whispered, "does it matter that he's a man?" "To my wife," "To my girl-friend," "To my nanna"; and so many of them, "To my mum." It was quite simply the most overwhelming experience I have had. To have been in a position to give these men a story of hope, to have been the means of connecting them to the story of my dear friend Lale, means more than I could possibly ever say.

I can think of no better way to end this book than with a short extract from my next novel, born out of that email I was sent out of the blue while I was in South Africa. It is a novel based on the lives of three brave sisters, whose love for each other helped them to survive the most appalling circumstances. The hope they held on to gave them the determination to wake every morning. After all, as Lale always said, "If you wake up in the morning, it is a good day."

Livia's Story

A death march through the countryside of Poland during the winter of 1945. The German soldiers marching the prisoners start to flee, aware that the advancing Red Army is now very close. Thirteen young girls break away from the group, leaving the columns of straggling, dying young women behind.

As night falls, they hold hands and run. There are still soldiers around, but it seems better to be shot in the back trying to escape than die from the cold and starvation. They soon find themselves in a forest. No shots have rung out, they have made it—away from the remaining SS officers and their dogs. The forest offers them no protection. The trees have been stripped of leaves, which now lie buried under the snow they struggle through.

Night becomes day, the sun blinding them as it blazes down, reflecting up into their faces from the snow on the ground. There are open paddocks now, some with livestock, cows feeding from freshly laid hay.

"There must be a farmhouse nearby," one of the girls says.

And now they can see a large house hidden by orchards and untended gardens ahead in the distance.

Following a path, they cross a paddock and head toward the house. One of the girls declares it looks like a castle, it seems so large and grand to them. They decide to ask for food and help from whoever lives there.

Making their way up the steps that lead up to the giant double doors, the boldest girl bangs the large brass knocker before stepping back. They wait patiently. No one comes. The others encourage her to knock again. Still no answer. They decide to look around the back.

At the back of the house they come upon the body of a man. He's dressed in fine clothes, but the bullet hole in his chest is obvious.

"We can't leave him out here like this," one of the girls says.

They decide to bury him.

They find shovels and spades in a shed. Weak from starvation and exhaustion, the girls take turns digging through the snow until they have a hole deep enough to bury the man. Working together, they maneuver him into the grave. They take turns saying what prayers they can remember, before covering him with dirt and snow.

Emboldened by having done the right thing, they try a back door to the house and find it unlocked. In the kitchen they discover a pantry filled with preserved food. Moldy loaves of bread tell them that the house has been empty for a while. Careful not to disturb anything, they continue to explore. Upstairs, there are enough bedrooms for each girl to have her own.

Finding their way back downstairs, they agree the owners would surely let them eat some of the preserved food, but it doesn't seem right to sit in the large dining room in a home that isn't theirs.

"Can we take the table outside?" asks one of the girls. "It's been so long since I sat at a table."

Double French doors open out from the dining room onto the garden, which looks out over the orchards beyond. Moving the table is a struggle but they manage to lift it and slowly march it outside and place it on a snow-covered patio. Returning inside, they each grab a chair. Lanterns and large candles in glass jars finish their table setting.

From the kitchen they bring plates, cutlery, and pre-served fruit and vegetables and smoked meats, which they carefully lay out on platters. In the pantry they find some cheese with mold on the outside, which is declared edible. One of the girls opens a cupboard and gasps in surprise when she discovers it contains bottles of wine. Carefully selecting two, she takes them to the table, along with wineglasses.

With the sun having gone, and the night sky filled with stars, the light from the lanterns and candles dances on the table in front of them. Thirteen young women who have survived hell on earth eat their first meal at a table in a long time. Once they have cleaned up, they discuss sleeping arrangements. Again, it is agreed they have no right to sleep in a bed which isn't theirs, but the owners wouldn't mind if they borrowed the blankets from the beds.

Each taking a blanket and pillow from the upstairs bedrooms, the girls lie down together on the floor of the dining room, in place of the table and chairs.

It is a moment of freedom for thirteen young women who have survived the unthinkable. Who knows what lies ahead, but for now at least they are safe, together, with a roof over their heads.

Acknowledgments

I wish to acknowledge and thank the readers of *The Tattooist of Auschwitz* and *Cilka's Journey* who reached out to me, by email, through my publishers, by attending a talk I was giving and speaking to me in person. It is because of you I have written this book. You shared with me your stories of hope, relating them to Lale, Gita, and Cilka. You brought me tears, you made me cheer for you as you bravely told me something deeply personal, trusted me to listen, and I did.

There are two people at my publishers who are responsible for this book. Kate Parkin and Margaret Stead, I owe you a debt of gratitude for your encouragement, your passion, your expertise, your love in guiding this book to the printers. It was as much your dream to write these words as it was mine.

I have mentioned them in my dedication but want to acknowledge further the staff, the patients, and their families and friends who passed through my life at Monash Medical Centre in Melbourne. In particular, Glenda Bawden. A woman of immeasurable compassion and generosity who I was proud to call

"Boss" for over twenty years. Your actions and deeds taught me how to care.

My daughter and son-in-law for allowing me to write something deeply personal and stressful about a time in their lives. I hope by sharing this, you will help others.

Livia, Pam and Oded Ravek, Dorit Philosoph, the families of Magda and Cibi for reaching out to me, opening up to me and giving me a reason to listen.

The wonderful people at my publishers Bonnier Books UK for taking a chance with this fiction author writing a nonfiction book. Perminder Mann, Ruth Logan, Claire Johnson-Creek, Clare Kelly, Francesca Russell, Stephen Dumughn, Blake Brooks, Felice McKeown, Vincent Kelleher, Elise Burns, Stuart Finglass, Mark Williams, Carrie-Ann Pitt, Laura Makela, Nick Stearn, Alex May, all the gang.

My friend, manager, traveling companion, she who makes me laugh, Benny Agius. We have had, and will continue to have, some wonderful adventures together. Thank you so much for everything you do for me.

I find my hope and inspiration in my family. They will always be acknowledged as the most important people in my life inspiring and contributing to my continued writing, my reason for living. My children, Ahren, Jared, and Azure-Dea. Their partners, Bronwyn, Rebecca, and Evan. My growing family of grandchildren, Henry, Nathan, Jack, Rachel, and Ashton. And Steve. I love you all so much. Thank you.

Further Reading

Julia Samuel, *This Too Shall Pass*

Lisa Damour, *Untangled: Guiding Teenage Girls through the Seven Transitions into Adulthood*

Philippa Perry, *The Book You Wish Your Parents Had Read*

Stephen Grosz, *The Examined Life: How We Lose and Find Ourselves*

Trish Gribben, *Pajamas Don't Matter*

Dr. Brené Brown, *Dare to Lead*

Dr. Brené Brown, *The Gifts of Imperfection*

Dr. Brené Brown, *Daring Greatly*

Dr. Brené Brown, *Rising Strong*

Dr. Bessel van der Kolk, *The Body Keeps the Score*

Matt Haig, *Reasons to Stay Alive*

Fearne Cotton, *Calm*

Fearne Cotton, *Happy*

Fearne Cotton, *Quiet*

Bella Mackie, *Jog On*

Bryony Gordon, *You Got This*

Suzanne Franks and Tony Wolf, *Get Out of My Life*

Anna Mathur, *Mind Over Mother: Every Mum's Guide to Worry and Anxiety in the First Year*
https://www.nhs.uk/conditions/stress-anxiety-depression/talking-to-your-teenager/